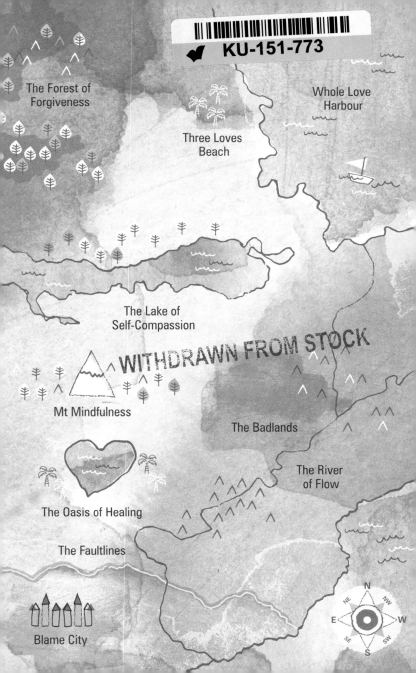

The Forest of
Forgiveness

Whole Love
Harbour

Three Loves
Beach

The Lake of
Self-Compassion

WITHDRAWN FROM STOCK

Mt Mindfulness

The Badlands

The River
of Flow

The Oasis of Healing

The Faultlines

Blame City

LOVELANDS

DR DEBRA CAMPBELL

hardie grant books

Published in 2016 by Hardie Grant Books,
an imprint of Hardie Grant Publishing

Hardie Grant Books (Melbourne)
Building 1, 658 Church Street
Richmond, Victoria 3121
hardiegrantbooks.com.au

Hardie Grant Books (London)
5th & 6th Floors
52–54 Southwark Street
London SE1 1UN
hardiegrantbooks.co.uk

A Cataloguing-in-Publication entry is available from the catalogue of
the National Library of Australia at www.nla.gov.au

Lovelands
ISBN 978 1 74379 270 4

Cover design by Michelle Mackintosh
Text design by Patrick Cannon
Typeset in 10/15 pt Calluna by Cannon Typesetting
Colour reproduction by Splitting Image Colour Studio
Printed by China by 1010 Printing International Limited

Some names have been changed to protect the identities of
the people involved.

Dedicated to all who journey.

Contents

It is the meaning we make of our experiences
that defines who we are and who we ultimately become.

DESMOND AND MPHO TUTU

1

—

PRIMAL LOVE

The heart breaks in so many different ways that when it heals, it will have faultlines.

JOHN GEDDES

As babies, our very survival depends on the fulfilment of a primal dream I call the 'bliss dream'. It's one of raw, sensual connection and soul-to-soul love where everything else is secondary.

When the dream is unrequited or simply imperfect, loss and disappointment can cut faultlines of anxiety, lack of self-worth or gaping emotional hunger in a developing heart. Even those who suffer little incur some losses as they grow – having to share parents with siblings, feeling pain, experiencing inevitable separations. Everyone has faultlines. It's part of being human. Some faultlines are deeper, more far-reaching or jagged than others.

Over time our faultlines are made raw, broken and etched deeper by stormy emotional weather; in other seasons their edges are smoothed or even hardened by our various experiences. Our early experiences influence how we see the world. Our brains unconsciously start to map out the potential paths we will choose, the kinds of people we will be attracted to and the emotional lessons and reparations we will feel drawn to seek.

From birth to death we define and traverse our Lovelands – our inner landscape of intimacy, passions and losses. It's through love that we pursue our most primal needs: the need to belong, the need for security, the need for a home, for sensual desires and the search for purpose and pleasure. All our reasons to exist live there.

Love is the pure elemental energy of life. Love is a sacred presence of mind, the highest quality of attention we need from ourselves and others. The fundamental goals of life are to realise that deepest energy and to embody it through the three great loves: compassion for our own soul, relationships and finding purpose.

~

This book started out as a memoir and a reflection on some of the most agonising and all-too-common causes of faultlines – loss, abuse and abandonment. I wanted to describe their effects on our unconscious mind, how this plays out in our relationships and how we can find healing. It became a richer manifesto on the many faces of love and how to find passion in life, love other beings fully and nurture deep compassion and caring for yourself.

Essentially, my story is a testament to the starring role of love in our lives, from birth to the legacy we leave after death. Love, particularly self-love, plays a larger part than we may understand or care to acknowledge in defining our personality, our identity, our relationships and the paths we choose. We each decide which interpretation of our experiences becomes our defining reality.

Knowing your Lovelands, your intimate inner landscape, will help you avoid negative patterns by recognising them and becoming empowered to make different choices when determining the paths to take on your journey. Whether you're a parent to others, a lover to another or working on the care of your own soul, *Lovelands* will help you make sense of love, from birth to death.

Through reflection you'll learn to see the past differently, more *usefully*, even the difficult parts. You'll acknowledge where you might have done your best at the time, even when things went badly. You will find forgiveness, humour and freedom from the past and acknowledge what you've learned. You will see where you've suffered and triumphed, choose what to make of your experiences and decide where to go from here.

Your struggles reveal your worth, your character, your unique constellation of strengths. Moving from struggle to insight gives you a new foundation to create the life and relationships you desire, and allows you to like yourself more. Knowing your faultlines is the first step towards freeing yourself from the pain of loves gone wrong, childhood scars and other hurts that might otherwise pull you down; so that instead, you can choose the path of self-compassion, greater emotional freedom and following your bliss.

You are the sovereign of your kingdom, your Lovelands. You have the power to make your meaning, tell a new story, re-author your world and map your future.

I'm a therapist and teacher, and I was once also a patient. I hope that by offering a no-holds-barred account of my faultlines and tracing the extraordinary implications they had for my life and relationships, along with the stories and triumphs of some of my patients and friends, you will feel less alone with your faultlines, whatever they may be.

I offer myself as a teacher, a case study *and* a friend to you on this journey.

Let's go.

2
—
LOST LOVE

Your absence has gone through me like thread through
a needle. Everything I do is stitched with its colour.

W.S. MERWIN

As a kid, when people asked about my father I said I didn't
have one. It felt true, although I knew there was a man
alive out there somewhere whose name I carried. He gave
me three years of sporadic contact and nothing else – no
goodbye, no explanation, no love.

Worse, I felt his abandonment as unspeakable shame.
If I had been prettier, a better little girl, my own father
would have chosen to stay rather than leave me, right?
That question haunted my subconscious for decades.

The fear that my flaws must be serious and obvious for
him to just *leave* cut into the bedrock of me. My inherent
unworthiness became an unquestioned 'given', as basic as
the colour of my eyes. Other girls were daddy's little one.

I assumed I was some kind of 'anti-princess' and I would have to cover and compensate for it for the rest of my life.

How loved or unloved we feel as children deeply affects the formation of our self-esteem and self-acceptance. It shapes how we seek love and whether we feel part of life or more like an outsider. Why wouldn't it? Our caregivers' responses are the clearest and most consistent feedback we have as we develop our identity.

My dad ran from his blinding fear and rage at finding himself stuck with a wife and child at nineteen years of age. So, like countless fatherless kids, I wore the tattoo of a defining abandonment that I believed my defects had caused. When the dream of love dissolves and we don't know who to blame, we usually secretly become our own prime suspect. Over time my pain calcified into the anxiety and shame of a kid who can't understand how they failed but believes they must have.

The last time I saw my father during my childhood, he came to pick me up in a brightly painted station wagon. We visited his girlfriend's mum. They were kind enough people, but Dad himself hardly gave me the time of day. He was already absent, but he hadn't told Mum or me how permanent and profound this absence was going to become. Although we hardly interacted, I remember feeling a sense of pride and childish ownership that day. I was proud to be in the same place as my dad, feeling accepted and valued by him, even after weeks apart. He took me back to Mum after a few hours, kissed my cheek and that was that.

The next weekend, Mum dressed me up in something special and told me Dad was coming soon. The time passed. I waited and waited and waited and waited. The time passed. I asked Mum why he didn't come. She told me the truth: she didn't know. He just stopped coming. It broke my heart.

That day was emotional Ground Zero for me. A deep faultline zagged through my inner landscape, obliterating the 'given' that parents *must* love you. My Lovelands were permanently scarred.

In the weeks following, there was no further information. Mum always seemed to be doing something else, something other than hanging out with me. I think she was trying to survive. She was twenty-two years old, alone with no support, broke and living in a tiny flat in a suburb where we knew no one.

Decades later, in therapy, I talked about that day. I remembered feeling the urge to go to the toilet and panicking that I wasn't going to get there quickly enough. I sat on the toilet for a long time, surprised that my undies were clean. It confounded my three-year-old brain to have clean pants because it meant there was no simple explanation for Dad's absence. If I had made some kind of obvious, dirty mistake I would have been able to justify Dad not coming to see me anymore.

Years later, I understood that I had formed a belief that day that I must have flaws only others could see. Those flaws, I believed, had led to this sudden and permanent rejection by my own father, my own blood. I felt shamed because Dad didn't value me enough to show up, enough to call, enough to even make up an excuse.

As young kids we unconsciously tend to assume our parents' failings must be about us because, for a while at least, our parents are godlike figures. We're hard-wired to idolise them for the first few years of life because we have to rely on them for *every* aspect of our survival. That's why we may blame ourselves rather than them for some of our disappointments, or for problems in the family that actually have little to do with us. It can be hard on our self-worth.

Our relationships with our parents or caregivers create an 'attachment style' – a blueprint for how we handle close relationships later. Attachment styles range from being secure and trusting to avoiding intimacy, or to experiencing mind-boggling ambivalence. Some people with an ambivalent attachment style become preoccupied with seeking love and attention and tend to feel power-less, needy and insecure in relationships. Others seek love vehemently, then run when it's returned or becomes intense because it feels dangerous to let someone get too close. Insecure or ambivalent attachment styles lend themselves to self-defeating patterns of trying to love while defending a heart that feels vulnerable.

This conflict between wanting to love and be loved *so* much, but getting sidetracked and screwing it all up out of a deep unconscious fear of loss is at the base of so much relationship pain and struggle. Of course, the self-sabotaging behaviour is usually unconscious, meaning we don't understand why we're doing it. The patterns were formed before we had words to describe what was going on for us. That's why they can be so hard to identify and forestall.

In my case, I became ambivalent about intimacy as a child, losing confidence in myself as lovable. I longed for closeness with others but felt afraid of being rejected again. I often kept to myself rather than reaching out to others because there was less risk of humiliation that way. My unconscious tried hard to work out how to secure love, how to be 'better' and how to avoid any further abandonments along the way.

I discovered early that pleasing others won praise. Pleasing others is great, but only if you don't negate your own desires in the process. It's too often synonymous with neglecting your own heart and feeling afraid to risk putting yourself first in life. Change starts when we realise that by diminishing ourselves we please no one. Yet it takes time to 'own' these aspects of ourselves, and it takes courage. The first step is to cultivate self-awareness, leading to the possibility of self-compassion and the building of self-worth.

Low self-worth early in life can lead to inadvertently choosing paths that erode our self-worth even further as we get older. Inexperience combined with intense need is a volatile cocktail. As life coach and author Tony Robbins puts it, we become obsessed with what we did not have. Seeking love, yet without reliable indicators of what it feels like to be loved well, makes you vulnerable to quick and dirty fixes of love that end up making things worse. It's hard to know what you're looking for when you've never seen it or felt it. You may repeatedly find yourself perched on unstable precipices of desire that you know are bound to collapse and hurt you at any moment. Yet there you are again and again, falling, wondering, 'Why?'

Ideally, a girl finds a positive role model in her mother's self-esteem, assertiveness and self-awareness in life and relationships. Then she knows what she's looking for when it's her turn. Similarly, supporting his daughter's attractiveness as a person and loving her without 'seductive' undertones is one of the core tasks of fathering. It's one of the factors that helps a girl grow into a balanced sexuality where she values herself and doesn't settle for whoever pays her some attention; where she can both love and desire another person without fighting through a wall of fear and insecurity every step of the way. It's the same for boys, only that being female adds a few extra cultural gender biases about sexuality and shame. It's still not the norm to call boys 'slutty' when they experiment with sex and intimacy, but for girls sexual shaming remains at the front line of verbal abuse.

I've heard a comedian crack a joke about 'page-three girls' being 'girls who weren't loved by their dads'. ('Page-three girls' refers to young females who pose topless on the third page of UK tabloid newspapers.) Although there are exceptions to every generalisation, the joke isn't too far from identifying an extremely poignant truth. People who have never felt fully accepted and loved for just being themselves tend to turn to whatever fulfils their hunger to be seen and adored by *someone*. It's as if getting some attention will heal the self-doubt and generate some self-esteem. But of course it doesn't work. Lust for attention at any cost just makes you vulnerable to exploitation and further damage.

Page-three girls are one manifestation of an emotionally doomed attempt to get some love. Showing your boobs will absolutely attract attention and might feel like a rush for a while as you imagine a life of Kardashian-esque fame and wealth. The trouble is, it's not the kind of attention that tends to develop into a deep and lasting sense of being appreciated, valued or even *seen* for who you are. Chasing quick and dirty hits of attention because you're hungry for love can get you hurt, and make you cynical and bitter after a while. You can only live off fast-food love for so long before your body and mind need real nutrition to keep going.

We go looking for love in all the wrong places because of fundamental misunderstandings about the nature of love, how it feels, and how to go about giving and receiving it. Predators can more easily engage targets who are longing for attention and desperate to be seen and valued by someone for something ... anything. The best protection is to prioritise love, acceptance, quality attention and compassion when we raise our children and in the way we treat ourselves.

Not all parents realise that just being physically present isn't enough, although it's a fine start. Love is essentially a form of focused and generous presence – a special kind of authentic engagement. Love is the highest-quality presence of heart and it's a gift that builds self-esteem. When, as a child, someone consistently indicates that you are worthy and good enough in yourself just how you are, this becomes a part of your reality as your sense of identity develops. While being physically present as much as you are able as a parent is important, it isn't enough without emotional presence, without engagement and an interested connection.

The consistent affirmation of your innate worthiness to be seen and heard serves as a platform on which to build your emerging impression of yourself. Unfortunately, many people don't receive sufficient or consistent engagement to help them feel acceptable and worthy in themselves as they reach adolescence and beyond. But regardless of the gifts you receive – or don't – from caregivers, eventually you have to take on the care of your own heart and soul, and determine what might need a bit of work.

Knowing yourself, building self-esteem and finding self-compassion are typically a few steps forward, a few steps back, but there are some steps that won't lead you astray. Keep developing the things you are already good at and the things you love so you spend more time in 'flow', or immersion, in a space author Gay Hendricks calls your 'zone of genius' where you're passionately living your strengths. It can take patience, I know, to stumble upon the things you love and the zone where you're brilliant, where time melts away into bliss. We don't always know our passions until we find ourselves doing them and realise we're totally in our element.

As well as patience, building self-esteem takes courage. Take some measured risks (nothing dangerous) but try things that push you out of your comfort zone. You'll feel proud of your courage and see that you are stronger and braver than you may have known.

Get physically strong because the process strengthens your head as well. Looking after yourself physically, giving attention to your wellness and self-care nurtures emotional strength and stability more than you might realise.

Building self-esteem and self-compassion requires deeper changes, too. If your self-talk, meaning the way you talk to yourself in your head, tends to be harsh and critical, it's essential to become aware of this and to start infusing some new ideas. If you're hard on yourself, ask yourself whether you'd speak to someone else that way. Would it help a child to grow in self-esteem if you spoke to them the way you speak to yourself in *your* head? If not, think about giving yourself the same level of kindness and compassion you'd give another, because feeling ashamed and criticised, for whatever reason, is hell.

Self-compassion is a vital ingredient in wellbeing. And, of course, it's a more palatable way of saying 'self-love'. Before we go any further into exploring these common faultlines, I want to be very clear about the difference between *blaming* and unearthing insights that facilitate change. Blaming your parents or someone else for your sadness or low self-esteem is not what I'm on about here. Blame is disempowering and paralysing.

Insight, understanding and awareness generate acceptance and fuel your journey towards emotional freedom. Insight means realising why things worked out as they did, why you are how you are, maybe why they were how they were. It's not about making excuses for anyone. It's about assessing the depths and locations of the faultlines so you don't keep falling into them for the rest of your life.

For some years I saw Colin, a patient who was racked by auditory hallucinations – a cruel, critical voice shouting venomous words at him in his mind. Despite the help of medication, he was sometimes driven to depression and desperate moments of grief that made him pull over his car and sob on the side of the road. He'd experienced scathing, relentless criticism and taunts from his father for as long as he could remember. His father had died many years before, but the abuse had cracked deep faultlines in the boy, which still groaned and gaped in this now middle-aged man's internal 'badlands'.

It was vital to Colin to *never* regard his father as a 'bad person' – so much so that he held on to his pain and rage at his father's cruelty, thereby creating an emotional pressure-cooker within himself. He (unconsciously) preferred to believe in his own unworthiness rather than accept that his father had been verbally and emotionally abusive and, like all of us, was a less-than-perfect human.

When he was able to name what had happened and acknowledge the consequences for his life, yet give himself permission to still love and believe in other parts of his father, Colin could begin a slow, steady walk toward greater emotional freedom and peace. The voices lost some of their sting and were quieter when they were present. More importantly, Colin became less afraid of them, able to hear them on occasion without being driven into panic.

Insight and acceptance of the past are empowering; internally handing back accountability is liberating. But again, this is not about blame.

Let's take a brief tour of Blame City: a soul-sucking town lit up with neon billboards that offer various poisons to fill the hole inside us or numb the pain for a little while. For people who get addicted, it's a hard town to leave because it's lazy and cheap.

But blame slowly drains you of everything – your passion, your strength, your authentic personality, your compassion and free will.

It's OK to visit Blame City for a while. Take the tour. A well-travelled path in the Lovelands leads to it and it's worth knowing your way around there so you don't get stuck in its mean, seedy areas. Be angry, be clear that you've been hurt and there are no excuses; but also be ready to keep moving.

You can't create a different past, no matter how much you would like to, but you *can* find the power to keep growing beyond *any* experience. There is a time to rage, to hide, a time to grieve – then the rest of your life to re-engage. Sometimes freedom starts with accepting that a horror really did happen but you aren't back there anymore. It's finished and it's time to decide where you want to go from here.

One of the most challenging things about the journey of healing from childhood losses is that our growth and development, even after achieving insights into what happened, are not linear. The faultlines that were cut into us can repeatedly intersect our path in many unexpected places. For example, the loss of a parent can be both physical and emotional; or perhaps your parents were physically present but emotionally unavailable or abusive. Whichever scenario, the loss of a parent or a significant carer during childhood causes multiple losses, not just at the moment of the carer's departure. I felt the loss of my father at every stage, at every special occasion he didn't mark, on every day he didn't turn up for the rest of my childhood and adolescence.

However, the greatest losses went far deeper than the loss of the man. It was the loss of *belief* that I was worthy, that I was lovable, that I was good enough. There was the loss of the *dream*, the bliss dream of being unconditionally loved by a father and sharing an unquestionable bond with a man. Then there was the loss of the *opportunity* to form an emotional map of what it felt like to be loved by a man, as a child, without sex or having to *perform* in any way.

Finally, there was the loss of *safety*. It's dangerous to go into the world and relationships with no map, no preparation, no safe place inside yourself to fall. The Lovelands are vast, the terrain so varied and the weather unpredictable. Every soul needs a map.

Each of us has unique circumstances, a different land-scape, but our Lovelands are always made of stars, beauty, pain and humanity. Our inner maps depict many of the same core features – they're just arranged differently. Each of us can be the hero of our own inner journey.

We're all born from the Sea of Bliss Dreams, hitting the physical reality of human frailty hard as we emerge from a warm, watery realm. The transition to earth and air isn't without challenge. We carve our inner landscape as the experience of being human unfolds.

Right from the start, relationships with others don't always match the bliss dream of perfect love we once wordlessly imagined. Losses and hurts become faultlines in the bedrock of our Lovelands. Some faultlines are tiny cracks, disappointments that cause a tremor but are quickly forgotten. Other experiences, such as abuses or losses, slice out a chasm that dominates the landscape. They become permanent and perilous unless we learn to map and navigate them with awareness.

Some of us get lost, repeating relationship mistakes; or we find ourselves going in circles, wandering inner badlands that feel like soulless wastelands, not understanding why we're so far from the dream.

Disappointed, we may find ourselves attracted to Blame City, broke, lost or addicted to something or someone we hope will ease our pain or ennui. You've got to grab your stuff and make a break for the River of Flow.

At the river you can immerse yourself in authentic pleasures that soothe you and allow you to leave dead-eyed distraction and compulsions behind. You'll feel your mind, soul and body being replenished on the River's beaches. At the River of Flow time disappears and life force comes alive. Flow feeds resilience – it's a lifelong source of soul nourishment. It's a haven to return to again and again, so explore it and identify your sources of flow so you can always return to them.

Life demands that we keep growing, finding our people, our work and passions. When your faultlines are deep and perilous, they block your progress, trip you repeatedly or keep you trekking round in circles in arid, desolate badlands. Look for the Oasis – support that is there in hard times, not only good. Find a guide or travel companion if you can; look for the well of your strengths and drink deeply.

A pinnacle will rise on the horizon, a place that's important to your own power and intrinsic wisdom. This is Mindfulness Mountain. We'll go there together.

The view over the Lake of Self-Compassion is breath-taking and a path leads right down to its lotus-covered waters. Here you'll find a new equilibrium.

With wisdom and mindful awareness, you'll better manage the Mirages – the distortions, dead ends and mistakes that are an inevitable part of any journey. Sometimes things turn out to be other than what you hoped they might be when you find yourself stuck in Projection Pass. Revisit the Lake of Self-Compassion often, return always to the River of Flow for comfort and pleasure. Drop your bucket into the Oasis wells and drink again. Then journey on.

Encountering the Plains of Uncertainty at some stage is a certainty in the Lovelands. The weather, the topography, the behaviour of others, random chance – these are things you cannot control no matter how well you prepare. It's likely in relationships and other areas you'll sometimes take a wrong path; your compass might be damaged or those damn faultlines will block your way.

Take heart, adventures must have challenges – it's part of being human and building resilience. In the end, how we respond to what happens matters more than what happens to us.

There's every chance the River of Life will wash you up on Broken Heart Beach at some point, sunburnt and thirsty. You might find yourself there a few times. There are cliffs of grief and hurt, twisted driftwood and countless shipwrecks on the rocks. It's a jagged and desolate place with thorns in the sand.

You just have to get up at those times, even if you don't feel strong enough. Remember what you're good at, remember what lights you up, remember the River, the Lake and the Oasis and start the trek back into the interior.

3

—

LOVE ABUSED

Out of your vulnerabilities will come your strength.

SIGMUND FREUD

I wasn't the only one who didn't know what a close, loving relationship with a male felt like. Many years later, I realised that neither did my mum, even though she was a grown woman who had married twice.

Despite Mum's father being a benevolent presence in the home, she felt little emotional closeness with him. He was unwell for many years, rendered withdrawn, quiet and breathless by emphysema. She did not really know him, and neither did I.

Apparently my grandparents didn't tell Mum about sex until it was too late. However, they did tell her to marry her boyfriend when she got pregnant at just seventeen years old. Later, as a single mum in her twenties, she didn't have a clue what to look for in a partner or how to create a relationship that would make her happy, so she fell for the first man who showed an interest in her and made her laugh.

Mum married ex–merchant navy man Gerry, hoping he'd be a white knight; but he was not the man she so badly wanted him to be. It could have been the opportunity I craved too, a second chance at a dad, but Gerry wasn't the daddy type. Right from the start he behaved more like a jealous sibling than a father figure.

One of Gerry's favourite 'games' was to trap my head between his thighs, towering over me as I sat on the floor watching TV or doing homework. He would squeeze my head just hard enough that it hurt if I tried to get away. He'd stand there leering, apparently getting something out of it – a short, stocky, forty-something hero overpowering a skinny five-year-old girl for kicks. I would yell for my mum, who generally wasn't in the room when he did it, but Gerry would convince her he was 'only joking'. She wanted to believe him so much that she did. Mum taking me seriously would have meant she'd have to get us out of there, so I had to put up with the bullying. For a decade or so.

Gerry was thrown from a car while drunk-driving in the days when seatbelts and sobriety were considered optional. He hit his head hard on the road and must have damaged his brain because he subsequently developed seizures. My mother could have died that night except she *was* wearing her seatbelt and ended up hanging upside down in the overturned car rather than joining him on the asphalt. Mum said Gerry was never quite the same after the accident and saw his head injury as the reason for his 'grumpiness', as she called it. Her hypothesis didn't really hold water though because prior to the accident Gerry was frequently rageful, impatient and given to violent outbursts. Apart from that he was a great guy. Apparently.

Gerry regularly drank to delirium, which was the reason for the accident in the first place. He had some very deep and ragged faultlines in his foundation. A country kid, I suspect he was abused when he was sent to boarding school at twelve, because he ran away from school suddenly at fifteen and would never discuss it or go back. Somehow he took himself to sea on a private merchant ship, regularly travelling to India, and slowly worked his way up to first mate over the years. Gerry's past was largely a mystery but he was clearly no stranger to violence.

When you have been brutalised and get free of it, you have a choice to make, if you are able to see it. Perhaps Gerry's choice was ultimately taken from him by his brain injury. I don't know. I do know that after abuse you eventually choose how to live and behave based on what your experiences have taught you. The options run from emulating the abuse in some form to rejecting all violence and preventing suffering wherever you find it. Or somewhere in between. We each make our choice.

Gerry didn't hit Mum because she hardly ever stood up to him like I did when he was rude, hypocritical or cruel. He hit me on the face a couple of times, kicked me in the back once when I was sitting on the floor and I didn't move fast enough at his command, but mainly he just yelled a lot. He had a vicious temper, something I'd never encountered in a person, so he was another shock lesson in men. He exuded a pervasive scent of menace that kept me constantly on edge, although I can only name it in retrospect. I learned to second-guess my every move, always unsure when I would incur the wrath of the ogre.

No one deserves to be treated like this, but since I tended to be a quiet little *pleaser* who largely kept away from him, I'd hoped it might make him go easier on me. It didn't. The lesson: abuse has nothing to do with deserving. It has nothing to do with who *you* are.

I also grew up feeling constantly sexually assessed by Gerry which, sadly, is not uncommon for girls. It was normal for me to feel shameful, like I had to hide myself because something was 'wrong' about Gerry's attention, especially combined with my pre-existing fear of not being good enough. Often I felt angry without any specific reason. It's difficult to question the world you're growing up in when it's all you know, but I worked out that dads aren't meant to be like Gerry. I could see others around me who were different but unfortunately weren't mine. Kris, my friend from primary school, and I spent many fun times with her family, going on holidays together. They weren't the perfect family, they had their dramas and disagreements like anyone, but it didn't escape me that no one ever behaved like Gerry.

Sometimes I tried to imagine having a gentle, loving, mature father-figure beside me in life to affirm my worthiness, to make me feel safe, to guide me on my way; but, having never felt it, as a child I could never get a sense of it. My dad was almost lost from memory, leaving the faultlines of shame and unworthiness to be carved deeper by life with Gerry.

Mum's devotion was misplaced on Gerry and she knew it quite soon, but she didn't want to fail again at marriage in her own eyes or, even more so, in the eyes of her loving but judgemental mother. She lived for her mum's approval above her own happiness. Mum felt shameful and guilty for her one big mistake of a teen pregnancy and accepted her 'punishment' without question. Although she was miserable, she dug in and held on to the relationship with Gerry like a life sentence.

There were gifts for me that came from the years with Gerry, but of course I wasn't able to integrate what I'd learned until long after he died. It took quite some time and a fair bit of therapy to get free of just plain hating him.

I abhor cruelty and bullying more than almost anything else, largely because of him. I probably even found my vocation as a psychologist because of Gerry. His rages, rigid thinking, narcissism and general undiagnosed mental illness meant I often felt more mature, self-possessed and wiser than him despite the fact that I was a kid and he was an adult. Whatever the reasons, I knew that I understood more about being a compassionate and loving person than that well-travelled man would ever know. I understood the vital importance of treating people with kindness and respect because he showed me how unbearable the opposite felt.

Often, I also felt tougher and wiser than my mum. Although I was very much a child and dependent on her for many things, I had stood up to the beast of Gerry alone so many times while she hung back. I saw his madness while she kept herself blind to it. After a while I understood that telling Mum how much I despised Gerry clouded relations with her but achieved nothing. She was all I had and it was better to shut up unless things were really bad.

I saw Mum as childlike, even lacking courage, and at times unintelligent because she subjected us to Gerry for so long. I was angry with her for Gerry for decades, but not anymore. Insight eventually cured me of it. Mum was neither stupid nor without courage. She brought me up lovingly, while dealing with her own childhood demons.

They kept her voiceless, frozen in an earlier time of her life and feeling powerless, withdrawn inside herself for longer than she could remember.

Mum had suffered sexual abuse from a teenage boy who sometimes babysat her. His mum had died after giving birth to him and my grandmother had taken him under her wing and had trusted him, but he had suffered terrible damage. By recalling events for which the date was known, Mum worked out that the abuse must have started when she was only three. It was unclear to her how long it continued, but she knew it was repeated.

He would 'examine' her genitals using a teaspoon with a tiny silver figure of a man on the end of the handle. Decades later she said that the physical discomfort inflicted upon her was less significant than the terrible betrayal of her trust and the emotional impact. The abuse led to her feeling shame, a sense of dirtiness about herself that she couldn't shake for years. Worst of all, it taught her that she was powerless over her own body, that she had no sovereignty over herself and no voice to speak out when she was being hurt and violated. Mum had little belief as she grew up that she was allowed to set boundaries. It was normal to allow herself to be led into things in order to show she was a 'good girl' who did as she was told, even if she didn't want to.

The abuse taught her that a person charged with caring and protecting could repeatedly hurt you and shame you into silence so that you believed there was nothing you could do about it. Her self-esteem was kicked repeatedly, and hard. Becoming a mother before her time, she could not help but model her low self-esteem, her lack of voice, her sense of powerlessness to me.

Trauma not only affects self-esteem, but can also change the patterning of neural pathways that affect how well we cope with stress, develop resilience, manage our emotions and function socially. Trauma can shape our core beliefs about ourselves, others and the world. This is often more pronounced if trauma and abuse occur during the early stages of childhood.

Somewhere in life Mum had also learned that it wasn't OK to be honest about your feelings if they were feelings other people didn't want to hear, if they weren't convenient and happy feelings. She had tried to tell a neighbour about the abuse but had felt shut down, as if the woman didn't want to know. She had never felt able to tell her own mum but she wasn't sure why. Suffice to say, she felt it would reflect poorly upon herself and therefore wasn't worth the risk. Hiding from genuine feelings if they were inconvenient and difficult, and instead pretending everything was rosy, became Mum's normal way of operating; a survival mechanism. Mum needed to tell herself we were a happy family, as though acting it out would eventually make it so. She modelled how to smile through clenched teeth at a demanding drunk, how to deny reality in order to stay in a loveless situation. Years later, I realised that she had inadvertently taught me a lot about acting.

So on the one hand, life with Mum and Gerry showed me that I had innate wisdom and knowing, revealed me as a strong 'old soul' who could see through the lies adults told themselves and the cruelties they justified. On the other hand, being more reflective than my parents, having insight but no power, no street smarts or autonomy was lonely, isolating and at times enraging.

In psychology, it's called 'parentification' when a kid is raising the adults emotionally, more than the other way round. The adult may be facilitating practical day-to-day life but the child is their confidante, helper and wise, overly responsible little friend. It's not ideal. Parts of childhood are lost and you constantly feel out of your depth in the world, not realising you shouldn't be asked to be all of those things before your time. It's tough, you tend to learn through rookie failures and moments of drowning panic, but for better or worse it can make you extremely self-sufficient.

Jax personified the losses and gifts of parentification. She came to see me, seeking respite from a hot mess of old and new trauma. Among her night terrors was a basket of venomous snakes that writhed around each other in her dreams, regularly jolting her awake in a cold sweat. She told her GP she needed more sleeping pills but he told her she needed more than pills this time and wrote a referral to me.

Jax had left a long army career which in the last few years had taken her on a peacekeeping mission in East Africa during dark times in that land. One hot dusk she'd heard shots coming from a position on the outskirts of the massive, overcrowded refugee camp where her unit was stationed. Someone was on a hill, taking pot shots at people in the camp below for entertainment. In near darkness, Jax found the person responsible – a teenage kid nonchalantly sitting on a rock with a semiautomatic weapon. After some heated words on both sides, Jax broke with protocol and slapped the kid hard across his face in blind rage. Jax ended up with an AK-47 in her face in return. She froze and waited to die. The boy laughed and ran into the night.

Jax's post-traumatic stress and insomnia were powerful and challenging to ease. It soon emerged that there were other, deeper layers to her faultlines – barely obscured old sink-holes that were opened up by recent events.

Jax began to talk about her childhood, growing up poor in the country, the eldest of four daughters of an alcoholic mother. Bingo, I thought, but not in a good way. Africa was not the beginning of her trauma, it was the last straw.

Jax had always been the peacekeeper, ever the protector, the girl soldier prising her parents apart from trying to kill each other and getting hurt herself. Throughout her life, she'd barely had a break from the job. In all her relationships, she was the rock. She was great at it, everyone depended upon her and she never let them down, but it burned her out.

Now Jax was lost, wandering the badlands, suspecting danger in every hollow, on guard every night, barely able to rest. Then, another landslide in the earth of her Lovelands occurred. Jax's mother died, setting her back again, making the terrain we had to cover even rougher.

It was a long road to an oasis in the desert for Jax, until she found Angie. She'd made it to the outskirts of her badlands, but Angie held out the hand that led her out along the shortest path. Love brought healing faster, closer. At fifty-three, the right partner changed everything for Jax. She was no longer alone in the small, dark hours.

Angie allowed Jax to see the world through a different, safer lens. At last someone Jax loved was equal to her in courage and self-sufficiency, offering *her* protection and asylum from pain, rather than the other way round. Angie bestowed on Jax the sweetness of life after war, the possibility of childlike fun, a safe place to fall that she hadn't known for so long. Nurture and protection for *herself* was an ancient, almost forgotten dream, not something she'd ever expected to experience.

With Angie she slept through the night for the first time since the army. She began to laugh instead of raging so often at the world. Through love the trauma shrank slowly, little by little. Raw, unremitting pain morphed into seasoned wisdom and self-compassion.

Unsurprisingly, it wasn't long before Jax got back to improving others' lives, consulting on infrastructure projects in developing nations. The vigilance remained, the faultlines sharp and never too far to see on the horizon; but Jax was happier, no longer imprisoned in a life-defining role that was imposed too early.

~

There are so many ways the faultlines of our parents can crack into chasms of our own as their experience of what it means to be a person and make relationships exerts its influence on us. So easily we can become lost, unconsciously following the default paths laid down in childhood, falling repeatedly into faultlines we cannot see. Insight, compassion and awareness allow us to begin to accurately map our Lovelands and signpost the faultlines for next time we pass. Awareness allows us the choice to define ourselves rather than being defined by what happens to us.

4

LOVE IN FLOW

Walking with a friend in the dark is better than walking alone in the light.

HELEN KELLER

Primary school was a good place for me. It was a small school and I was part of a streamed, tight-knit little group of high-achieving students, kept together with the same teacher from years 4 to 6. Never underestimate the importance of a few quality role models – they can make a huge difference to a life, even when their involvement seems small. School was safe, stable and engaging when my home life felt illogical, disconnected and lonely.

My pal Kris and her family regularly went camping, often taking me with them to the coast. Kris and I are like cousins – different parents and homes but a sense of coming from one soul family because of a deep shared history. We grew into very different people, yet have a constellation of uncanny similarities. It all started back on the beach where we'd spend hours, days, roaming unsupervised, but never knowing any troubles, only adventures.

The limitlessness of the windswept beach was the opposite of the home I lived in: a two-bedroom, ground-floor flat – dark bricks, maroon nylon carpet and tan vinyl. The beach was a pure escape to freedom. Such experiences are treasures that broaden an otherwise small and limited perspective and inspire passion for living. It's important to connect to those passions as early in childhood as possible because the experience of *flow* through passionate engagement reaches deep into the core of human wellbeing.

'Flow' is a term used in psychology to describe 'being in the zone' – when all thought and emotion are harnessed to one thing in the moment, which is intensely satisfying and enjoyable. It feels like all the parts of yourself are connected and working together in total immersion in something you love while everything else fades into the background. It's an intrinsically healthy, supportive and natural zone where your personality is shining at its brightest and it feels amazing. On the map of the Lovelands, I have named it the River of Flow; perhaps you've been there? Its valley is verdant in all seasons, a place of life, teeming with ideas and inspiration, a place to return to without limitation – every single day if you choose. Its waters are always plentiful and rejuvenating.

Experiences of flow give meaning and purpose to everyday existence. Flow often comes when we rediscover a captivating and joyful experience from childhood. Such an immersion can strengthen our mental health and point to potential paths of purpose and fulfilment in our adult lives.

Kids are great at it but work and the responsibilities of adulthood can take us away from the daily experience of flow. That's why it's useful to look back at your childhood for clues to those experiences of immersion, if you have lost touch with the doorways into it. Your treasures, your soul-feeding passions, may evolve as you grow, but you may still get a hint from what once nourished your insides.

Experiences of flow show you how you can be your own friend, deeply enjoying your own company and illuminating the areas of genius you can offer the world. Flow experiences are exercises in kindness to yourself, so they encourage self-respect and develop your strengths, satisfaction and happiness.

I first became consciously aware of flow, the bliss and love of life, at the beach. Kris and I loved horses and we galloped imaginary ones endlessly up and down the sand from dawn till dusk, never getting tired of it, barely noticing the fading light. We would make up their names and pretend all the details of looking after them, from riding them to dealing with the imaginary dramas of the stables. I also loved dogs and I dreamt of the day when we might be out of the flat and I'd have the space and lifestyle for a canine buddy.

I also found flow in ballet classes. I loved the exercises at the barre where, after a while, I could trust that my body would pick up the rhythm and join with the piano and the chant of the teacher: 'Up, point, close.' Years after I gave up ballet I missed it still. I learned that it's important to stick to your passions even when it becomes challenging to fit them into life because if you let them go you may regret it for years.

Music was also important to me. Lyrics gave me a sense that other people knew how I felt because empathy was lacking in my real world. Music was an escape and refuge for me, as it is for people universally.

Yoga was my most important place of flow in my senior years of school. I loved dance but yoga was a physical expression with a deeper and more connected purpose; less artistry, but connection of mind, body, breath and awareness. It gave me a sense of unity, energy and confidence. It helped me to feel healthy, strong, comforted and supported by a tradition much larger and older than myself, which is exactly what it's supposed to do. I loved to think about how, for thousands of years, someone, somewhere was meditating or doing some yoga practice, at any given time.

Discovering the pursuits that give you a deep sense of engagement often marks the start of feeling empowered, purposeful and back on track in your life. Over the years I've met so many patients and others who have found the experience of immersion in their passions to be profoundly life-affirming, even life-saving.

Patsy lived through events no person should face. When I met her I immediately recognised her name and then her face, older but distinctive, from media coverage of years before. The kidnapping of her eight-year-old daughter Eloise was a case burned into our collective memory, blazed across every newspaper and screen. I was the same age as Eloise when it happened and I lay awake in fear countless nights after the girl was taken from her bed not all that far from my suburb.

Decades later, when we became friends, Patsy told me that the loss of her child almost killed her. When she held up a faded front page against her chest, a wave of sick horror washed through me. I could barely think of such loss, yet here was a woman who had been forced to live through it. How had she coped?

Patsy is a painter and seamstress. For decades she's made and sold unique artworks blazing with primary colours, full of hope.

She told me how through the stitching, stitching, stitching by hand, by night and by day, somehow it helped her hold herself so tenuously together. Somehow she would find a way to immerse herself just enough in something beautiful to survive another day, to push hell back a few centimetres overnight. Stitch by stitch, day after day.

Flow can be a powerful ally in self-care and a place of intense creativity and inspiration. I've known numerous people who do their best thinking on long runs or find meditative flow in swimming laps, coming out feeling balanced again if under stress. Authors, bloggers, even journal writers, may describe their writing time as sanity-preserving – as their self-care as well as their art, passion and work. Writing has been my lifeline in times when I could not understand how else to process what was happening to me.

Every landscape is nourished by a River of Flow and it's part of our journey to locate and map our paths down to the water and dive in whenever we can. Author David Whyte observed that the antidote to exhaustion isn't rest, but wholeheartedness. In times of exhaustion, confusion and grief, immersion in flow can be one of the most effective lifelines to vitality and resilience, the most direct pathway through the badlands of emotion that we all trudge across at some point. It's powerful, self-generated natural medicine.

Knowing your passions, knowing flow, knowing how to be *with* yourself in positive ways means having a solid, untouchable backup plan: a first-aid kit for mind and soul when the inner landscape gets emotionally ugly or down-right dangerous.

5

—

FALSE LOVE

Maybe you are searching among the branches for what only appears in the roots.

RUMI

As a teenager, my faultlines began to exert their influence on my landscape's wider horizon. That's how life goes: our early experiences influence how we 'attach' to others and who we're attracted to, for better or worse. Knowledge is the map to freedom from old patterns – but I knew none of that yet.

The private girls' school I moved to at Year 7 was strong on religious dogma and academic achievement but low on social and emotional support. I think we all found it pretty cold. But it did offer opportunities to try new activities that weren't available at my old school, like taking part in plays. I was excited to realise how good I was at pretending to be someone else with a different life, mimicking emotions and accents. Best of all, when I performed I got lots of compliments and attention from girls and teachers who otherwise wouldn't have noticed or spoken to me.

When I discovered acting and the massive rush of approval I got from performing, I believed I had found my life's vocation. It happened when I was thirteen. Applause felt like the acceptance, popularity and love I hungered for. When people were impressed with my performances I felt like I was *something*, good enough, special. A classic introvert performer, I was paradoxically full of courage performing for a few hundred people but terrified of being looked in the eye one on one.

It was freedom and relief to pretend to be someone else, to tell myself a story that changed daily mundane details into something fascinating and exotic. Walking to school, I imagined I was navigating busy Venetian canals in a boat. I created fantasy family members and mused about how different life would be if they were real. I went through a phase of telling stories about meeting someone famous or doing something cool that hadn't really happened. Kris, who knew my life too well, would know I was lying but she usually didn't say anything. Probably because I was the only kid in our fancy school who was living in a dogbox with a crazy stepfather, she cut me some slack for wanting to be someone else.

I met James, a trainee actor from a drama school, when he was directing a play at a local theatre. I was in Year 10, sixteen years old. James was eleven years older, sharp and experienced in life. I looked up to him as friend, mentor and sexy, protective older man. He saw me as a virgin schoolgirl fantasy to be had.

Mum was immediately suspicious of James but I gave him my complete faith. I didn't know how to work out whether a man cared for me or wanted to have sex with me, or both. I had no role model of being loved by a male to measure him against and, truth be told, I craved his attention so much that I barely cared what I had to do to keep it.

James wasn't around as much as a boyfriend normally would be; but then, he wasn't a schoolkid boyfriend. I was so excited that he was interested in me and wanted to hang out that I didn't question his whereabouts the rest of the time. He would pick me up from school, we'd spend a couple of hours talking, watching TV or going for coffee, then he'd go home, staying under the radar of my mum and stepfather, who were at work until 6 pm.

We started having sex gradually and not for a year or so. By then we had developed a genuine friendship and I absolutely trusted him. I was listed as an actor by an agent who started to get me some work and James was loving, helpful and gave me loads of tips and support.

Looking back, I can see that James was grooming me as his young lover, as a virgin girl to take when the time was right, for a couple of years. All I can say is that life and love are complicated and I felt genuinely loved by him as well as, well … used. There is no love and consensual sex in which we don't, to some degree, use one another for pleasure – it's all a matter of degree, of whether the love is there in the ways that matter. I don't think he had intended to fall in love with me at the start and stick around, but that's the way it had gone. Unfortunately, even when James was in love he was still a player.

When I finished school I was accepted into a drama course with the ambition to be an actor still burning strongly in me. James had moved from an outer suburb, where I had never visited, to the inner city and I spent a lot of time at his apartment with him. My stepfather hated James and thought it was a good idea to throw me out of home because I wouldn't stop seeing him. Everyone warned me about the difference in our ages and experience, but I knew that James loved me.

It ended with James after I found a letter to him from a casting agent we both knew. She wrote about her love for him and her hope that they were not 'just a fling'. It smashed my heart and sent me tumbling into the fault-lines in my inner ground. As it turned out, James had been sliding from one strategic sexual conquest to another, seducing casting agents with considerable success, building his career and his ego. James wasn't a victim of the casting couch, James *ran* the casting couch. Much later, I understood that there were a number of women who believed they were 'the one' for James.

After we broke up, a mutual acquaintance told me that until he moved to the inner-city apartment, James had been living in the suburbs with a wife nobody in the acting industry knew existed. I was broken-hearted, ashamed and felt so stupid to have had no idea. My belief in myself as a judge of character took a massive hit when all my defence of James blew up in my face. I'd been the 'other woman' in my first-ever relationship without ever having a clue; but in retrospect, how could I have known? I had no experience, no knowledge of relationships with men and a deep, urgent longing to be loved.

We make poor choices of partners for many reasons, reasons that are as much about us as the other person. The topography of our Lovelands – where our faultlines lie, the depths of their chasms, the raw sharpness of the rocks, and how well-equipped we are for the journey – all play a part in our susceptibility to getting it wrong. That being said, there are some traps for young (or older) players that even some emotionally well-equipped travellers frequently fall into.

A big hazard as we traverse the Lovelands is finding ourselves lost in the narrow, maze-like reaches of a gorge called Projection Pass. In this context, projection means that, without knowing it, we project our fantasies onto a new or potential lover as if they were a blank screen showing a movie of our bliss dream. For example, my mum projected all her hopes for a happy family onto

Gerry and by the time she came to her senses and realised he was not the kind of person she had wished for at all, it felt too late to leave him.

We watch a new lover with excitement and the expectation that they'll fit our dream script of what we want them to be, more or less. It's all unconscious, of course. When they do fit our dream, we love it. When they don't, we try to minimise it, at least for a while, telling ourselves that the misstep was probably an isolated incident and they will still turn out to be all we want them to be.

When you wonder what a friend sees in their new lover who seems so obviously wrong to you, it's possible that they're seeing something very different. They're focused on a projected fantasy version of their lover that is not apparent to anyone else.

For a couple to traverse Projection Pass, they must pass through a shadowy gorge, highly vulnerable to being ambushed and trapped – in this case by an unwanted version of reality. If things go awry, they may become aware of the mismatch you and others saw all along and question their choice of travelling companion. But generally this does not happen until the veil of projection lifts. It takes a while for the couple to clear the pass and get back onto open ground where they can see the world and each other more clearly.

Projection often occurs during the 'limerence' or 'falling in love' stage of a relationship where hormones and arousal run wild and reality takes a back seat. We only start to let ourselves accept the disappointing ways our partner doesn't fit our dreams a little further down the track when the blind rush of limerence has settled down. That's why taking some time to get to know a new partner before re-arranging your journey around them is so important. You need enough time for the limerence to pass and for the reality of the other person to come through.

It's also important to force yourself to listen to the small voice of knowing behind the projections and hopes you have about a partner, and not overlook glimpses of who they really are if you don't like what you see. It's possible to get stuck wandering in and out of Projection Pass for years if you try to hide from the truth.

The second trap so many of us are ambushed by when choosing a partner is not understanding enough about who *we* are to know what's going to work for us in love and what's just going to smash us. Making good decisions depends on self-awareness – knowing yourself, knowing the faultlines and the strengths of your inner landscape. Lack of self-awareness is the food of dysfunctional patterns. Sigmund Freud was a genius in positing that until we know ourselves better and consciously bring to light where we are going wrong and why, we're likely to keep repeating familiar, self-defeating patterns, trying to make it right *this* time. Our unconscious hope is that we will fix things eventually; but we're unlikely to make a better choice if we haven't achieved the insight and self-knowledge necessary to change our perspective and methods.

That's why self-awareness and self-compassion are the keys to developing greater wellbeing, self-esteem and better relationships. Freedom is being able to liberate yourself from unknowingly repeating behaviours that do not serve you, that are self-sabotaging, often without you really understanding how or why. Freedom is choosing a different route through the Lovelands where you consciously avoid the crevasses and faultlines carved long ago.

Sometimes you *do* realise you're making the same kind of lousy choice over and over, but a familiar kind of bad feels so good that you push aside the suspicion that a relationship is likely not a good idea long-term. You get drawn in repeatedly by the misconception that you can play on the edge of a dangerous precipice and not fall into the crevasse *this* time. You take the same risk again and again, hoping to achieve a different outcome despite the odds being against it. That rush of familiar pain when you hit the ground reminds you of where you came from and it's perversely reassuring.

That which feels erotically charged is powerful, even if the lust comes from longing to fix something that can't be fixed; the hope that you just might attain the unattainable *this time* is intoxicating. James, my first love, was a classic daddy substitute gone wrong.

Jax, the career soldier, was attracted to needy women who lusted after a powerful, protective partner. She was a charismatic dream lover for a lesbian damsel in distress. The relationships were erotically charged at first with the ecstasy of fulfilling complementary desires, but Jax would typically become resentful and want to move on. Hearts would be broken, faultlines exposed and she would be lonely and lost in the desert again, not understanding why she did what she did. Try as she might, she couldn't find a place to be her full self in those hot, unequal relationships. When she had to be the carer there was no place for her to be vulnerable without fearing she would lose the respect of her partner and herself.

When Jax began to understand more about caring for herself and naming the qualities she longed for in a partner, she was able to find whole love with Angie. You repeat some lousy, self-defeating patterns until you understand how to stop.

Again, it takes time to discern if there can be genuine caring *and* powerful erotic connection with a potential lover or whether you're in a self-destructive cycle, lured by the siren song of the old pain your unconscious yearns to heal. A good clue is that a combination of friendship-love and compelling eroticism is ideally satisfying for most long-term lovers. Keep an eye out for that sublime combination and know that it can take a little time to walk through Projection Pass together and determine whether you're likely to have that experience with someone.

Another tripping hazard on the journey lies at the opposite end of the spectrum from dangerous erotic charge: making an overly safe choice of lover at the cost of a sufficiently interesting, sustainably erotic or passionate connection. Choices made out of fear or a need for security, that put aside passion, are rarely our best or most sustainable choices of lover.

Finally, intense neediness, for any reason, tends to lead to rushed decisions and subsequent regrets. Trying to fill a love-shaped hole with whatever you can stuff in it because it hurts so much usually leads to wrong decisions, exhaustion and hopelessness. One of the most challenging and ultimately rewarding tasks in the journey is to stumble upon contentment in our own company. As we've discovered, the River of Flow is one of the best places for unearthing that treasure.

If you're struggling to find love, don't get stuck in Blame City, believing the fault lies in your past. Finding the right partner involves some luck as well as effort, but it's the kind of luck you can go a very long way to influencing.

Know your joys, know how to fire up your passions, live the values you admire in people and *be* the love you want to feel. Most of all, be kind to yourself. Finding self-acceptance means you can contain your longings and take your time making connections with others that are real and fulfilling. You can take your time because being alone with yourself and your personal passions is far from a bad place to be.

Which of the mistakes in choosing a relationship have *I* made?

Why, all of them!

Of course.

6

SERIAL LOVE

A mistake repeated more than once is a decision.

PAULO COELHO

In my twenties I was looking for love above all else. I stumbled and fell into potholes and even chasms along the way as I felt very lost. My faultlines seemed to constantly crisscross my path and it was hard to get clear. I met some fun, inspiring people and I met some really difficult ones who pushed me deeper than ever into my internal chasms. I met people who were dealing with faultlines a lot nastier than mine, people balancing on precipices, playing with drugs and other crazy demons. Some of them moved to Blame City or disappeared into their badlands and I didn't see them again.

I left drama school to take a dream acting job with one of the two biggest professional theatre companies in town, as a lead in the Harvey Fierstein play *Spookhouse*. It was a rare achievement to get such a great start and I thought I'd made it big with all the attention. It was a fantastic experience that all my drama school buddies would have given a body part to have. I was lucky and on track in my career, I thought. But I didn't know about the industry, the necessary networking, bitching, fighting and schmoozing. I lacked contacts, street smarts and strategy in the dog-eat-dog insular world in which I found myself.

Mostly, I had difficulty discerning friends from 'frenemies' – people who want to be around you when it seems you're doing well but run when you fail. I was usually unable to identify them until I found myself feeling used or dumped. When *Spookhouse* ended and I flopped in a few auditions, I was unemployed. Life between jobs was unstructured and I felt vacuous and unmoored.

I'd thought being an actor was my path to self-esteem, but it quickly became a nightmare of rejection and self-doubt. It got to the point that even if I had an acting job I didn't feel excited by it after the initial thrill of 'winning' the role. I gradually lost touch with love for the art because it wasn't feeding me the self-acceptance I was trying to milk it for. I was hit hard by bouts of anxiety and a new, creeping self-loathing because I would sabotage my efforts without understanding why I was doing it. I 'acted out' my rage at myself by failing auditions through lack of preparation or by running late.

It's tough when you're somehow supposed to know what to do in life, but you don't; and while you're bumbling around trying to work it out, people twice your age, or with twice the industry smarts and connections, want to eat you alive. Many years later when I was a therapist with twenty-something patients, I referred to this time as the 'quarter-life crisis'. It's often the time when unresolved childhood hurts and low self-esteem come home to roost, negatively influencing the way you think and behave as an adult.

Twenty-three-year-old Stella was my patient for a year. Withdrawn and disconnected from pleasure and flow in her life, she came to see me for help with depression and crippling anxiety. Her quarter-life crisis was raging and her faultlines were potentially lethal crevasses. Stella was chronically lost in her badlands and frequently suicidal.

Online was the only place Stella got any approval or positive sense of connection with others. She was from the country but shared a tiny city flat with her brother. They were both on welfare and didn't get on too well. She played World of Warcraft night and day, barely ate any real food and slept only when she had to. Her teenage years had been so painful that Stella had withdrawn into an alternative virtual universe; but a year after quitting her retail job and trying to make it as a professional gamer, she was running out of money and getting sick. Past grief and abuse tormented her and she became afraid to leave the house, developed anxiety tremors and felt wordless and sad most of the time.

Depression entered Stella's life like a ghost, invisible but palpable. I imagined it lowering the temperature of the air as it glided in beside her. Her depression was like frozen rage held down so hard its gnarled features were no longer recognisable as anger – only as heaviness, absence, emptiness.

Stella stopped shaking after a few sessions and her vicious self-criticism calmed a little as she gradually became more mindful of the ways she spoke to herself. We explored the enormous guilt and shame she'd been harbouring for years about so many things. She spoke at length of the bullying she'd experienced in high school and its effects on her. Gradually, with a great deal of encouragement, she began to experiment with re-engaging with the world. Come on Stella, I would hope silently, come out, connect with me, find a way, little steps.

During one session our conversation turned to gothic fashion. We mused about the glamour and likely discomfort of corseted gowns and agreed that post–corset era fashion was better for breathing but nowhere near as romantic and fantasy-provoking. By the end of the session Stella was giggling shyly and smiling – so lovely, a pale cyber beauty, flowering as the icy pain thawed under the warm sun of loving attentiveness to her soul. She so needed a friend. Then the session was over and the haunting spirit hooked its wiry arm through hers and glided with her from the room. The cold sadness made me shiver.

After a few months of slow improvement, interspersed with some numbed-out weeks of obsessive gaming, Stella announced that she was going away with her brother to the beach, without a computer. She seemed quite calm about stepping away from her online world for a while to try other things again. When she returned from the holiday she said she'd been listening to music she loved but hadn't played for a long time. The music, although melancholy, made her feel happier than she had in ages. I loved that she was finding pleasure and flow in something, anything.

Her faultlines got a little precarious for us sometimes but Stella fought her numbing demons to engage with awareness rather than go dead inside under stress. She gradually learned mindfulness and new ways of caring for herself physically and emotionally. Most importantly, she started to forgive herself for all her perceived imperfections, the time she had wasted and the mistakes she felt she had made. She started to release herself from her world of shame, step by step, and her ghosts slowly faded away.

She found experiences of flow in reading and blogging and didn't play Warcraft all that much anymore. Stella left therapy for a job as a nanny in an outback town in northern Australia. They didn't have good internet, which both excited and scared her, but she'd decided to tough it out. Last I heard, she was considering studying to become a teacher and she was still working with children and enjoying it. Stella had found a path in the real world of her Lovelands as well as in fantasy by accessing flow, finding the courage to reconnect with other people and allowing herself a little compassion.

~

When I was about twenty-two, some neighbours at my inner-city flat introduced me to a guitar player called Joey, and we rushed into a heart-wrenchingly romantic relationship. Watching him play at bars enthralled me and I couldn't wait to be his girlfriend. I knew it was going to happen. He sang to me from the stage.

I soon found out that getting involved with Joey wasn't my greatest idea. Taking your time is one of the hardest things to do in relationships, but it is necessary to preserve mental health. Generally, if certain basics aren't good at the start of a relationship when things are at their most exciting and fresh, they're unlikely to improve when the novelty wears off. This especially goes for the erotic vibe between people – if it isn't strong on both sides at the start it probably isn't going to be any stronger a few months or years down the track.

Joey lived and breathed a hundred per cent rockstar. He was a talented guitarist and singer but he didn't have the genius level, or the luck, to stay out of cover bands and keep his own band going. He'd been signed to a record label and had some moderately successful releases but he'd struggled to come up with a viable album and the deal had fallen through. As a respected session musician, he was well-connected and successful and he enjoyed easy days and lucrative nights with way too much female attention.

These were my clubbing years. I worked in nightclubs, played in clubs and breathed their cigarette smoke and ugliness almost every day. Staying up all night serving drinks was hard work but I pretended to like it because it was cool and I needed the money.

Joey was physically gorgeous, kind, gentle, and he whispered to me about everything romantic, everything I wanted to hear. I thought he was the god of coolness and love. He liked me a lot too, but something wasn't right. We got deep into the heart of the Lovelands too quickly, crashing into Projection Pass so blinded by guitars and glamour that I didn't see rocks tumbling from the sheer walls of the gorge until they started to block our path.

It turned out Joey was great at starting out on romantic, passionate journeys but he wasn't good at leaving the Pass. He wanted to live there – swept up in the magic and exhilaration of falling in love, unable to let it turn serious. He was living the classic Peter Pan life, forever a gorgeous child by choice. He wanted a relation-ship, but not the grown-up kind I wanted with him that involved adult stuff like a home, a shared world, some kind of plans. I was in pieces when I lost the dream of Joey because I had seen him as perfect and he was undeniably beautiful, in body and soul.

It's clear *now* that I was serially attracted to men who, for various reasons, were 'unavailable' (funny about that with my dad being such a man) but I didn't see the pattern back then. How could I? It was going to get worse before it got better, as things often do.

Furthermore, it emerged for me much later that I was attracted to men with narcissistic qualities. The boy-friends I chose tended to be charismatic, needy, low on empathy and grandiose in their opinion of themselves. It seemed natural to pander to such men as I had seen my mum do it with my stepfather almost all my life. It seemed normal to try to please, to accept second best and seek approval; but I also knew it was pretty soul-crushing. It's just not that easy to create a whole new normal when you only know what you know.

Soon, a chain of career train wrecks, sprinkled with a few victories, lay twisted in my speedy little wake. In relationships, I concluded that intimacy was not my superpower. Working in clubs, I knew many faces, but I was close to very few. I met Pete, an actor, on a tele-vision commercial shoot. Pete was true to my pattern of attraction: a little on the narcissistic side. He was incredibly charming and appeared sensitive and caring at the outset, but he could shape-shift from an agonisingly sensuous Adonis who made me feel adored to a self-obsessed energy-vampire in sixty seconds or less. He was unpredictable and distracting at his best, heart-breaking and abusive at his worst. Another fabulous 'unavailable' love choice.

When he could no longer pay his rent due to unemployment, I let Pete move in with me. Major mistake. I was yearning for Joey, or at least a version of Joey I could have a sustainable relationship with, and struggling as an actor to survive financially. Pete sucked me dry on both counts.

Like me, Pete was spending most of his time as an unhappy camper lost in the badlands, with mature intimacy well beyond his capacities. He is the only person I have ever known to masturbate over a photograph of himself – the embodiment of a narcissist: in love with his own reflection. I walked in on him doing it. I know, right? So why the hell did I like him, even love him?

Great question.

Remember what I said about eroticism? For many people, agony and ecstasy get mangled when we're falling over old faultlines. We're unconsciously trying to heal or make sense of the pain of the past so we find ourselves intensely attracted to potential partners who will enact the other role for us – the role of the one who hurt us.

I think this best explains why we find ourselves desperately and repeatedly attracted to unavailable, abusive or unsuitable partners. A part of us is trying to repeat what we know until we get a better result, not realising that the way to get that better result is to wake up to the fact that we're whipping a dead horse and we need to cut our losses right *now* and pursue a better deal.

For example: if, like me, you're attracted to charisma, adventurousness and power in a man but you also want to feel secure, it takes a special combination of characteristics in a partner to fit that wishlist. To avoid barking up the wrong tree, it's vital to look past limerence and projections to assess whether a charismatic wannabe partner is also capable of empathy and consistency.

As I found in my relationships with James and Pete, some of the qualities that are most magnetic to us can sit right on the edge of our biggest faultline, which is *precisely* why they're so exciting. But it all stops being exciting and turns into hell after you've smashed into the chasm below so many times you're in a lot of pain. You've got to have the patience to look beyond hot, edgy and desirable for what you need emotionally, which, for most people, is a combination of trusting love and erotic attraction. You have to keep your eyes open and stay mindful through Projection Pass so you can check your map, read your emotional compass and see where you've emerged when you hit the full light of day again.

Don't give up on hot and edgy – but don't take it when it's *all* that's there, and end up repeatedly short-changing your soul. Most of us need and want someone we trust on the end of the rope when we risk everything around our sharpest and most dangerous edges.

~

My stepfather died of cancer when I was in my twenties and after a while Mum relocated to the country with a younger man she'd met through friends. I suspect she was trying to recoup some of the years that mothering me had stolen from her since her teens.

Mum loved me in her own way, which at that time pretty much involved cooking biscuits and staying away from anything sad; she liked to keep things full of sunshine. I understand now that's how she survived abuse; but back then, before I knew it, it made me angry. I felt she just left me to drown in my Nirvana-fuelled angst, and in Pete. Her pain from childhood kept her partly frozen, unable to fully grow up; but the flipside of her pain was her skill at shutting down hard when the going got tough. I envied her childlike naivety at the time because it allowed her to feel joy over the smallest things, things that gave me nothing.

Pete and I lived together for some time, struggling to stay afloat financially with sketchy acting jobs and supplementary work. I barely earned enough for the bills and Pete earned less. He came from a country Catholic school background where some ugly stuff had gone down in his childhood. I gradually realised that he was stuck in the past more than I was and he was really afraid of life. I was lost for direction now that my brilliant career had soured and I just didn't want to be alone. I didn't understand that I could ask more of my life and go out and get it.

I frequently worked all night and slept all day. I became pregnant due to carelessness and when Pete was unsupportive it finally dawned on me that maybe this wasn't how love was supposed to feel. I broke it off with him but kept letting him come back again and again. Drowning in debt, anxious and feeling very alone, I lost the baby. I was in trouble inside myself, deeply lonely, sad and grief-stricken in a way I had never before experienced. I hadn't been ready for a baby but, more than that, I hadn't been ready to lose one.

I stayed with Pete much longer than was good for me. I felt so alone and my self-esteem had slipped a long way through being an actor in a severely limited industry. Besides, it was the grungy, dark '90s where self-loathing was considered downright artistic. Think the Seattle sound, Soundgarden, Nirvana. It wasn't bright and breezy but that's how it was. I still wear mostly black. Enough said.

Unlike almost all of my friends, I didn't play around with drugs. I did yoga instead. Don't get me wrong, I didn't take very good care of myself, I just didn't take all the illicit stuff my friends were into because I was afraid of the myriad possible consequences – a criminal record, death, or a life of addiction being the main ones. I don't really know how my friends managed to overlook their fears, ignore their conscience and indulge. I guess they were just bigger risk-takers than I was.

Gradually, predictably, I sank into depression. My life felt so messed up at twenty-six. I wanted a clean one without the losses and dumb choices. I wanted to get a new life where I had self-esteem, where I had a clue. I secretly longed for a cool dad figure to help me recognise dangers before they smashed me, and to love me despite my faults and confusion about almost everything.

I occasionally started to find myself thinking that my life was complete shit. Looking back, I can see that it really wasn't that bad. I was just lost – no map, dysfunctional compass, wandering in circles in the desert badlands. I sank into musing that being dead couldn't be all that much worse than continuing the life I had, which felt devoid of meaning and purpose. There was not much emotion in my suicidal thoughts when I had them. They felt flat, factual, emotionless.

Slowly, insidiously, my thoughts became dominated by a sense of failure, anxiety and depression. I hated being like this and I hated myself for not being able to fix it, so I kept spiralling downwards. In retrospect, I can appreciate how serious the situation was becoming and how much I needed help; but at the time, it was hard to see anything clearly through the fog of depression.

I realise now that buried beneath my listlessness and depression was epic rage at myself and my circumstances as well as the frustration of not knowing a way forward. I felt so disempowered and lost that I couldn't see what I needed to do was to tap into the energy of my rage at myself and the world and channel it into something, *anything*, positive. It tantalised me that the only way out of the desert was to hurt myself. The paths to the River of Flow were overgrown and disused and I could rarely find my way to its water.

Now I know that the way out is not through hurting yourself or anyone else but through passion, like plugging a dormant appliance into a socket. Ultimately you can't rely on love from another being to save you because that's not something you can control. Although it's brilliant to have support, and indeed I recommend it, nobody can do your inner work for you. You need to find love for your life again. I needed to hack my way through those over-grown tracks back to the valley of the River of Flow, back to passionate engagement with my own world.

The problem is, this isn't simple when you're depressed. It means putting one foot in front of the other daily to get help and to focus on two kinds of experiences as much as possible: activities that evoke your flow and passion, as we've discussed; and activities that promote your sense of mastery or competency. If nothing is working for you, get help.

I knew I couldn't keep trying to figure out life and relationships alone for much longer. I was going around in circles, unable to escape and running out of energy. I didn't have any idea how to find the love I longed to feel, but an optimistic spark of hope on my dark horizon kept pulling me forward. Something in me believed I could turn myself around and map a course to somewhere better. Something was telling me that it wasn't time to give up yet even though I sometimes wanted to.

I took myself to a random doctor and sat sobbing in shame at the juxtaposition of my 'potential' and my reality. The doctor looked at me pityingly then consulted a list and gave me the names of a couple of therapists. In his referral letter he wrote that I was chronically low-level depressed, grieving the loss of a pregnancy and had a failed acting career, leading to financial distress.

'Failed acting career'. What a bizarre thing to write about me at twenty-six years of age! I guess that sums me up, I thought miserably: every life area in chaos.

I called the therapists' numbers in the hope that some-how I might manage to create a better life if I could make sense of my jumbled insides. I was flying blind but the way life was going I figured I had nothing to lose by asking for help. So I presented myself for 'professional help', having no idea what it actually was or how it worked.

I didn't expect what happened next, or how this decision would affect the rest of my life in extraordinary ways, good and bad. Done right, therapy can alleviate pain and suffering, and even transcend death through its ripple-down effects on subsequent generations liberated from dysfunctional family patterns.

Effective therapy has a number of ingredients, but includes one essential core ingredient that is subtle, volatile and dangerous to work with, but impossible to work without. It's love, of course. I call it a dangerous ingredient not because of what love is. Love is the simple and pure elemental energy of life. It's a sacred presence of mind, the highest quality of attention we need from others and ourselves. The danger, as I've mentioned, is that if we don't know the real deal of how it feels to be loved in early life, we ache for that love so badly that we can lack discernment about where we get it. We may go looking for the perfect love to assuage our yearning in all the wrong places, including in therapy.

Good therapy is healing; yet paradoxically, it's also where projection and fantasy run wild because you can know little about your therapist's real life. In the absence of reality, your imagination fills in the gaps about your therapist in idealised ways.

For a while at least, you may put your therapist on a pedestal because they provide a glimpse of longed-for compassion, caring and acceptance. However, it's *you* who must embrace the wisdom you gain there, map your faultlines, journey your inner landscape and become the hero of your own life. Taking responsibility for where you came from, who you are, who you want to be, then heading there is the heart of the hero's journey.

7

—

HEALING LOVE

The meeting of two personalities is like the contact of two chemical substances: If there is any reaction, both are transformed.

CARL JUNG

On TV, I heard life coach Tony Robbins say that growing up with someone like my stepfather can ultimately make you a stronger, wiser, more aware person once you get far enough past your pain and anger. I wanted that to be true for me, but I didn't know how to bring about the shift.

I got the idea of therapy from Woody Allen movies and watching *Oprah* because at that time I didn't know anyone who'd been in therapy. Oprah had suffered abuse far worse than anything I'd encountered and she had come through winning in life, so I took her as a personal-growth role model. A part of me felt embarrassed to ask for help because going to therapy was not as mainstream as it is now and I certainly didn't think I was 'sick' and needed a doctor. I wasn't sure if I was doing the right thing by going, but I didn't know what else to try.

I knew my depression stemmed partly from a lack of meaningful purpose in my life – the quarter-life crisis – as well as from my romantic disasters. I was directionless in life *and* love and I felt like I was just wasting time rather than living. I wanted to understand what purposes my life could serve that would be engaging and fulfilling, as well as useful and wanted in the world. Acting already seemed like a frivolous and unrewarding waste of time because the industry was fickle and shallow, characterised by rejection and periods of unemployment.

Aside from career, I wanted to experience a good relationship and a strong sense of belonging. I just had no idea how to achieve those desires since I seemed to be getting relationships so wrong. I was sad about how my life was unfolding; but more than that, I was deeply frustrated and angry with myself for not knowing how to change it. That's really what prompted me to go to therapy.

First I called the female therapist I'd been referred to but she had no appointments so she suggested a colleague named Josh. He had space to see me the following week so I booked in, hoping to find some relief from myself. I arrived wearing cut-off jeans, black tights and lace-up boots: more rock'n'roll than hooker, but trying to look downright tough, attractive and edgy. That was just me back then, trying to be liked. His consulting rooms were in a small house not far from the beach, accessed by pushing the doorbell and waiting to be admitted; but I got there nervously early and the previous patient let me in on their way out.

Big mistake.

Things didn't get off to a comfortable start. We looked at each other and something jagged through me like lightning, from him to me to earth before I could blink. Nothing like it had ever happened to me before. It was somewhere between an intense déjà vu and a freaky feeling of 'I know you from somewhere', but his face was not familiar and I am certain to this day we'd never met. He had almost unbearably intense blue eyes, which made me fall apart, just a little.

While I was reeling with whatever the hell had just happened, his first words to me were, 'How did you get in here?' delivered with penetrating suspicion.

I was horrified, stuttering, embarrassed as I tried to explain. Great start. He thought I was a mad stalker. Finally, we sat down in his enormous black leather chesterfield chairs and he began to interview me, poker-faced, showing no sign of emotion for the rest of the session. I bit my nails compulsively, dropping the torn and broken fragments on myself and on the chair the instant he looked down to write, then pretending nothing had happened.

After his considerable assessment across three agonising sessions that I attended only because I felt so desperate, he agreed to be my therapist. The process of psychotherapy he offered was over years, not months, although he could not say how many. Appointments would be twice a week, lying on a couch in the psycho-analytic style, and the process would likely produce deep positive change in me and in my relationships by helping me come to terms with the old hurts of childhood and almost 'reparent' myself.

It was not what I had expected. I had imagined doing a few sessions, focusing on dramatic, practical solutions to my problems, Dr Phil–style. I hadn't considered undertaking such long-term personal development–style therapy, but Josh presented a compelling case as to why it might be the best thing for me.

Therapy, especially long-term therapy, is not everyone's path. It's possible to work through the difficult parts of your Lovelands in many other ways and to find friendship, love, healing and support in diverse places, both known and unexpected. It's possible for some people to ease emotional suffering through relatively simple, meaningful changes in perspective and through developing new emotional habits. However, for some with a penchant for analysis, like me, long-term therapy can be a good fit.

Over the first months of therapy I catalogued my anxieties, frustrated ambitions and my bad boyfriend decisions. I offered up my sadness, my insecurities and my existential fears, all for Josh's scrutiny and with the hope of some help. The therapy room was an alternate universe – all about him and me. It was terrifying for the first couple of years, but, later, just the kind of universe I came to like most. Here was someone who wanted to listen to me; I did not have to perform. Here was someone who really heard what I said, and what I'd meant to say, even when it came out confused. It felt like a new experience because I was free from the judgement I'd always felt when expressing myself to others. It was OK to just be me.

A useful therapist functions as a guide to help you return to the River of Flow, to explore more of its streams and access ways to nourish your soul. I began to discover, or rediscover in myself, passions of my mind and heart that would eventually become very significant in my life.

Some years into therapy, my interest in the world of mind and emotion led me to return to university to study psychology. I developed an intense desire to understand people's behaviour and unconscious motivations. Psychology was a part of acting that I had loved, but therapy took this interest to a much deeper and more useful place. My new perspectives and self-understanding inspired me and made me feel more connected and alive to the world.

I likened finding feelings of purpose and flow again to dragging myself out of my arid desert badlands towards an oasis nourished by life-giving springs. In my mind the oasis has deep, palm-shaded rocky pools and warm sands by day; and clear, magical starry nights. It's hope, love, beauty and soul nourishment, even surrounded by anger, sadness and difficulty. In the midst of the deadening badlands, it is life.

There are many forms of healing oases. Each soul's Lovelands has its own unique landscapes, its faultlines, its soaring natural beauty and changing weather patterns that affect the environment within. For my patient Anna, the healing oasis was a real place she found – a stream tumbling over rocks into a verdant valley in the Scottish highlands.

'Drop your bucket in the well, Anna,' her mum would say when Anna was feeling anxious, sad or lost. 'You have more strength and genius in you than you know.'

After her mum died those were the words Anna held closest to her heart and rolled repeatedly around her mind. Was she living the full strength and potential her mum saw in her? Was she even happy, or was she just living?

The loss of her mother rocked Anna to the core, an earthquake shook her Lovelands, unsettling the foundations of everything she loved and thought she could rely on to be there always. The quake was devastating, the rebuild slow and painstaking, as grief often is. Intimate losses permanently reshape our landscape, opening old faults, forging new scars and sometimes revealing the rich ore and gems that lie hidden at our core.

Anna took a trip alone for the first time since university, since marriage and kids and adult responsibilities began to crowd her life. She wasn't running away. She only *half* wanted to go because everything she loved was at home. Anna told me she wanted to force herself to be alone for a couple of weeks, to remove herself from distractions, from her identity as wife, teacher and mother – to see what was left. To drop her bucket in the well.

Her mum was from Scotland so that's where she decided to go – to a guesthouse in the highlands in the thaw of early spring. Each day Anna hiked kilometres with her camera, finding cottages, villages, a church and a wood. A sense of home surrounded her in that strange land and she felt that some healing might come through time alone to feel and walk and drink in water and air.

On her second-last day, a local woman gave Anna directions to a valley where a stream originated from underground: a pristine, icy and whisky-ready cold spring. She sat on a rock and tasted the water from deep in the earth. The chill of the artesian water jolted her fully awake, shivering and invigorated, her skin buzzing with the air and space of the highlands.

She felt peace and mother love all around her. She felt at home inside and out. In that moment Anna knew that she was *enough*.

~

Good therapy is one oasis of life, a space dedicated to tuning into your inner world and honouring your feelings as real. Pain, shame and fear lose some of their power to intimidate you when you speak them and find that you're still accepted. A good therapist will know how to hold the rope, encourage, guide and support you when you decide to abseil crevasses to explore how your faultlines were created and how far they reach.

Josh helped me to map the beauty and treachery of my faultlines and negotiate the badlands from a safe place that wasn't about blame or inadequacy on anyone's part, but about insight and acceptance of the past and its natural sequelae.

For example, he affirmed that I was not responsible for the loss of my dad and that being scarred by such a loss is normal. He helped me to accept my faultlines of abandonment and low self-worth as understandable consequences of significant losses and not as random flaws in me. Understanding why my badlands formed as they did helped me to see the beauty in their desert-like landscape. Mapping that terrain has made me fitter, stronger, braver and a better guide to others.

8

—

MINDFUL LOVE

Mindfulness gives you time. Time gives you choices. Choices, skilfully made, lead to freedom. You don't have to be swept away by your feeling. You can respond with wisdom and kindness rather than habit and reactivity.

YOGI GUNARATANA

In my late twenties my yoga teacher encouraged me to train as an instructor and within me a sense of greater meaning through helping other people in a deep way began to emerge. I studied yoga and meditation – 'the art and science of stilling the movements of the mind' – instead of scripts and, unsurprisingly, I found yoga much more rewarding than acting. It wasn't just the physical side of yoga that I enjoyed; it was primarily my discovery of mindfulness that was life-changing.

Mindfulness can be defined in many ways but probably the simplest definition comes from therapist Jon

Kabat-Zinn: 'Mindfulness is the awareness that emerges through paying attention on purpose, in the present moment, and non-judgmentally, to things as they are.'

You can access an understanding of mindfulness best through meditation, but it is how the practice translates into the rest of life when you aren't meditating that increases resilience and improves all aspects of your existence. It was a big day when mindfulness hit me as an actual, possible way of life.

I'd been studying yoga and meditation for some time and I had the *theory* totally down; but apparently it hadn't really sunk into my heart and gut. Then there I was, one hot day, driving in outer suburbia, pretty uninspired, when mindfulness suddenly became my superpower. I was about twenty-eight years old and there was nothing specifically wrong in that moment. However, I became aware that I was involuntarily taking part in a self-made walk of shame – mindlessly berating myself in my head.

The narrative comprised memories from childhood through to recent times – mistakes, humiliations, injustices and hurts – and the swirling clouds of bad feeling emanating from them felt like stinky but *comfy* old clothes. I suddenly saw that when there was nothing else playing in my mind, they were the fillers that I had on an automatic loop.

Revelation.

My comfy self-loathing playlist was so familiar that – BAM! – like the proverbial 'emperor's clothes', when I recognised it, it became obvious. As the ol' parade cranked up that day and the shame and disappointment started to rise, I felt a shock right to the base of my spine. I understood that I could stop this.

I realised that I am the being who observes and responds to the workings of my mind. I am not the thoughts in my mind and I am not my feelings. I finally understood the teaching I had read and heard so many times. It was like waking up to a new world.

Don't get me wrong: mindful awareness wasn't an instant cure to my every difficulty, but it formed the foundational understanding that I had more power over my mental and emotional wellbeing than I ever thought was possible. My realisations that day catapulted me forward in my resilience and ability to manage my emotions and self-talk. They spurred me on in my yoga and meditation and helped me to embrace a more mindful way of living every day.

Mindfulness increases resilience because it gives us a way to be with how things are, to find some serenity at best or greater tolerance at least around aspects of the present that we cannot change. We get stronger by becoming aware of our thoughts and feelings, accepting their existence, but not fusing with the stuff that provokes pointless stress, self-destructive behaviours and unhelpful patterns of thinking. Instead of running unsolvable questions over and over in our heads, with practice we can exercise more choice about where to direct our attention.

For example, fast-forward to now. As part of his work my husband must travel overseas. Often I go with him but at other times I can't and, irrespective of the overriding sense of security I feel in his love, in his absence I find myself revisiting my badlands. This, despite the fact that life is wonderful, I have love around me always and I know I'm safe. Even though it doesn't last long, it defies logic to find myself stumbling around my abandonment faultlines like a lost child, peering into the dark, tempted to dive into melancholy and self-doubt as soon as my husband leaves the country.

Love, grief, self-doubt, abandonment fears – all emotion has its own logic, but its roots can be so deep that trying to explain it away in the conscious, brightly lit realm of thought and analysis isn't always enough. Its genesis lies in the primal realm of attachment, sensory memory and identity formation.

As with the distressed child who originally felt these things, gentle, loving presence can be more soothing in the heat of resurgent pain than worry and self-analysis. Mindfulness means giving this gentle, loving presence to yourself and others.

In times of stress, the thinking or 'doing' mindset can become a state of constant frustration or sadness because of our fixation on closing the gap between how things are and how we think they should be. There's an impulse to get rid of the pain any way we can, to fill the faultline in forever, obliterate the past. The pain in our Lovelands is experienced as more real and attention-grabbing than what is actually happening in the outside world, and we get stuck in distressing feelings that may not have a strong basis in actuality.

When the badlands beckon against all logical sense, I can tell myself that all is well; but feelings move in us beyond words, sometimes rendering them insufficient. Alone in the small hours, I have found that more is needed than positive self-talk, more is needed than words of assurance from myself or another. More is needed than therapy alone could provide. I need my own loving presence to give me courage. I need to make my way to Mindfulness Mountain.

How? For a start, by being present with what is happening and simply observing your body, thoughts and feelings. I generally turn my attention to my breathing first, deepening it to calm my nervous system and to connect my mind and body by giving them that shared point of focus. The 'being present' state is having nowhere to go, nothing to do. It is not goal-oriented or concerned with problem-solving. Being present to yourself can be dedicated purely to the processing of moment-by-moment experience.

In 'being' state, thoughts and feelings are events of the mind that arise, become objects of awareness and pass away, like noticing a sound that comes to your attention and then is gone. In this state, thoughts and feelings can exist without you taking any action. This means that mindfulness can reduce impulsive behaviour, such as addictions designed to increase 'good feelings' or get rid of 'bad feelings', by teaching us to tolerate 'unpleasant feelings' without jumping into 'get rid of it' mode or numbing out. Practising mindfulness strengthens the 'muscle' (metaphorically speaking) that lets us bear the discomfort of unhappiness, panic, anxiety and other difficult emotions without going under.

You can learn to shift out of 'thinking mode' into 'being' or 'observing mode' at will through quietly, non-judgementally watching your thoughts, feelings and the sensations of your body on a regular basis. Use your breath as an anchor when your mind starts to wander – keep coming back to observing your inhalations and exhalations. All you need to do is keep gently guiding yourself back to observing the breath and the passing parade of inner sensations, thoughts and experiences. Each time you get distracted and start wandering off in your head (at first this will happen constantly) just guide yourself back and start again. Starting over again and again isn't failing, it *is* the practice.

Time spent on Mindfulness Mountain can illuminate that you're the embodiment of a wiser, more constant presence than the ever-changing weather of your emotions would have you believe. You are like the sky. Your thoughts and feelings are like clouds. Breathe into the spaces between the clouds and let those moments of nothing-but-sky expand and remain your focus. In this way you will understand that you can identify with and always be comforted by the constant, calm presence of your core.

We are not problems to be addressed or sentences to be corrected. The faultlines have a beauty and history that reach back before words. They must be honoured. They can't be completely talked away, although this can help. They won't be bulldozed into non-existence. The past that put them there cannot be changed. It can be tolerable, even good, to sit with the faultlines, with ourselves, in the courage and grace of *being with what is*. Although the cliffs of the faultlines are dangerous, their genesis holds many clues about our personality formation, the wisdom of our feelings and some cautionary tales.

Mindfulness is a way of living with more awareness and less judgement, connected to a deeper sense of self. In great panic and anxiety, alone on a cliff face, it can be the cable that holds you from plummeting and that gently reels you up from a fall.

~

Alex was a twenty-five-year-old artist living a rock-band lifestyle with his girlfriend – sleeping by day and editing an online art zine and playing gigs in alternative music venues by night. His face was pale and adolescent, his hair too black to be natural and he regularly wore a long black overcoat that disturbingly reminded me of Columbine. He came to see me with a referral from his family doctor that described general, pervasive anxiety punctuated by inexplicable and debilitating episodes of panic. When a panic attack hit, Alex couldn't move, couldn't think and he felt so afraid that he feared he'd lose consciousness.

Alex was in the thrall of fear *of* his fear, every attack spiralling him deeper into a crevasse that seemed to have no bottom. We worked on disarming the panic, undermining its power to intimidate, practising mindfulness strategies as a form of emotional first aid that I hoped would become a source of ongoing resilience. At the same time I wanted to understand something of what was behind the panic attacks – to explore the crevasse with a torch once Alex felt brave enough to go in there by choice.

The reasons for blinding panic attacks are not always straightforward or one-dimensional. Seemingly inexplicable attacks can be a kind of unconscious smokescreen, a defence mechanism gone into hyperdrive, so overwhelming that they have become a problem in their own right.

In other words, the attacks may serve to obscure whatever's on the other side, something our unconscious feels we cannot look at. That being said, rarely are there tidy tracks that lead to an obvious culprit lurking in the shadows. Often the origin of the attacks stems from a combination of factors or from being under too much stress for too long. An exhausted soul's fight or flight mechanism may mistakenly smell unseen danger everywhere, becoming hyper-vigilant and increasingly activating false alarms of panic with little or no reason.

Alex and his father shared a fraught and volatile relationship in which his dad had long regarded Alex as an annoying little brother rather than as a child to guide and protect. Alex remembered watching horror movies with his dad from when he was only ten years old. Afterwards Alex would lie in bed full of terror, wishing he could un-see some of the images he'd watched; but they were in his mind's eye. He had needed protection and guidance from his dad, not to be made afraid without the resources to deal with his fear. Now similar feelings of vulnerability and terror were coming through in his adulthood, but Alex was no longer worried by the disturbing images.

He told me that those movies had awakened him to a dark side of human nature and a fascination with making graphic, macabre visual art characterised by torn bodies, death and autopsy images. The problem was that his fetish for the macabre disturbed even him, especially since it was the only kind of art he really wanted to make. His fascination caused him enormous anxiety.

Gentleness and slow, careful steps are needed in such unstable and dangerous areas of the Lovelands; move too fast and loose boulders can cascade down the slopes. Alex and I began gradually turning over some rocks and peering down a few overgrown paths of his inner landscape, picking our way, stopping to breathe and rest. I regularly reassured him that he wasn't going crazy with his ongoing panic. More than once I reminded him that the monster you think you see behind the bedroom door when it's dark generally turns out to be your robe hanging on the hook when you turn on the light. It's the same with panic. It feels like it's going to kill you with dread, but it's bluffing.

During one session Alex proudly showed me photos of his latest art work. I was chilled, but I didn't flinch. For an instant, I felt intense anxiety wash over me but I focused on Alex and remarked on his obvious talent. I thought of Warhol, my favourite artist's car-accident and electric-chair series. Art is meant to provoke emotion, I told myself, hold fast. Fear is contagious. I couldn't get spooked by the images and still do the job.

Alex was dark, but he was soft and childish and he seemed to need reparenting very badly – not from me, not even from his dad anymore, but from himself. I was determined to show him I could stay steady in the face of whatever tormented him so that he could be steady too.

I went down into the crevasse beside him week after week to explore it, search for what was emitting the waves of panic, wonder about the conflict-laden images and test hypotheses for easing his distress.

After a few months of progress punctuated by some difficult days, Alex arrived for his session looking pinker than I'd seen him and standing straighter.

'What's happening?' I asked him.

'I sat through the panic attack and did the breathing and mindfulness and I felt like it didn't have me anymore,' he said. 'I wasn't so scared. I felt like I could protect myself and I knew for sure the attack wasn't going to kill me.'

Slowly, the attacks reduced for Alex in both intensity and number, give or take a tough day from time to time. Alex described never having felt protected by his father, indeed feeling called upon to be confidant, emotional supporter and carer to his father for as far back as he could remember. He had been left alone to deal with normal childhood fears that attentive, sensitive parenting could have assuaged *and* he'd been handed the extra burden of adult problems and emotions he did not have the capacity to bear.

Over time we unpacked his burdens and left a few at the Blame City tip. Mostly, we focused on developing a sense of safety and a feeling of being protected from within – of being fathered emotionally for the first time. Moreover, Alex developed the courage to be with the feelings of each moment. His art continued to evolve, still dark, but Alex took on a new manliness, a new sureness of step. As winter faded into spring, he lost the overcoat.

~

Mindfulness helps you find the capacity to be with the inevitable pain that life dishes out. Of tremendous value to me was finding such a practical everyday way to become less afraid of my depressive and anxious demons that drove me relentlessly back to my faultlines. I had found a way to make friends with every part of myself and see every thought and feeling as an event, neither good nor bad, unless I decided it was so.

Ascending the slopes of Mindfulness Mountain offers a magnificent view that you don't get from the ground: a whole new perspective. Never had I had such a sniff of freedom. Never had I seen such opportunity, possibility even, to love my mind and myself in all my aspects, including the flaws.

9

—

FANTASY LOVE

I felt it shelter to speak to you.

EMILY DICKINSON

I was trying to break up with Pete when I started therapy but I was having trouble letting go and finding the courage to be alone. During one session my therapist subtly let it be known to me, not in so many words, that he suspected I'd be better off alone than with Pete.

I challenged him with, 'But the trouble is that if I break it off with him I'll just end up going back.'

All he said were three little words: 'If you wish.'

That was it. His ordinary words were strange magic that plunged me into a realisation of my power and responsibility for my choices, for my life. I abruptly saved myself from any more struggles over Pete on the strength of those three little words.

It was scary to experience a man as so powerful in my life, so necessary for my wellbeing; but the relief I felt to have Josh there as a guide was life-changing. The sense of security I felt with him disrupted my familiar ambivalent attachment style – so happy, yet so scared of loss. It was a level of relationship with a male that was unprecedented in my world at that time. My holy grail.

We spoke about almost anything over the years – the past, the future, psychodynamics of daily interactions, my studies, my relationships and feelings, feelings, feelings. At times he helped me to rehearse strategies for being more assertive, for communicating more openly, for retiring my self-defeating tendencies. He helped me to understand the family context I came from and its influences on where I was now. I began to see new possibilities of where I could go.

Having spent much of my twenties without a strong sense of myself, a complete overhaul of my identity and values felt necessary to me. My personality slowly, at times agonisingly, evolved.

My ambivalence about being an actor gradually resolved completely. I understand now that I love the arts but acting was not my vocation. After many years of conflict about what I wanted to be, it dawned on me that I'd become an actor because I needed to be seen and heard as a human being. I had not known how to achieve this in an intimate, personal way so I had performed.

When I was seen and heard by my therapist, and consequently by myself, I no longer desired to perform for attention and applause. I understood why I had sabotaged my auditions with lateness and lack of preparation. I realised that there was a part of me that deeply resented having to perform in order to be given attention (or love) and that I hated being judged and often rejected. That part of me no longer wanted to feel she had to dance like a circus monkey for love and was pulling me towards a more authentic self-expression, and a more satisfying and meaningful vocation.

It's exciting when you hit on a real insight that explains a pattern of your thoughts or choices that seemed so nonsensical but suddenly make sense. It resonates right through you and you suddenly realise that you now have the tools to initiate real and permanent change and growth. You generally know when a hypothesis or idea about your possible unconscious motivations is true or whether it's off track because you feel it right away. Your body feels alive, your mind feels like it flicks on a switch and illuminates a *bingo* sign. You've mapped a faultline, you know how it was formed and where it tends to show up. *Now* you have some power to navigate around it rather than falling in it and getting hurt.

I was grateful for the unprecedented peace each new insight brought me. I was grateful to Josh for helping to set me free from the limitations of my past, from the limitations of my mind. He modelled faith in me so I could locate faith in myself.

I saw in Josh a rare role model of a grown man. He showed strong ethics, he was disciplined, and he was successful and intelligent. He was always immaculately presented and his rooms were beautiful and home to a collection of stunning glass artworks whose crystal curves evoked the nearby sea. Above all else, he was more aware of and interested in the emotional journey of people, including myself, than any man I had ever met. He helped me to find kernels of meaning and truth beneath rubble heaps of confusion and camouflage.

Importantly, he did not insult my critical intelligence with forced positivity. He let it be so when things were deeply sad, unfair or enraging. He let the hot, angry truth be the truth, even when it was anything but comfortable to do so.

No wonder I fell for him.

I began to have recurring erotic dreams of Josh that reverberated in strong feelings in my waking awareness. It was pure desire for soul fusion and raw sensual pleasure. Week by week my faultlines were being explored and mapped a little at a time and the ancient bliss dream of perfect, soulful love glinted like a mirage in the desert.

Later I learned that my desire for Josh was laden with 'transference'. Transference is like projection, the trap for young players I mentioned previously, in which we believe that someone is precisely who we *want* them to be and transfer feelings onto them according to our fantasy image.

It happens to a degree in most relationships: we entertain assumptions and hopes based on our own experiences until we learn more about the other person. However, therapy provides the conditions for transference to occur more intensely and unequally than in other relationships, and for it to continue over time, because the therapist intentionally reveals little of themselves.

The goal is that, by not knowing about the therapist's real circumstances, the patient's imagination will unconsciously transfer onto the therapist the roles that will help the patient simulate the kind of relationships they need to understand or heal. The relationship between a therapist and patient is unlike other relationships in a number of important ways. The feelings of love and caring that can develop on both sides, borne out of deep trust and intimacy, can be every bit as intense and overwhelming as 'real world' love. Yet the feelings exist in a temporary relationship where there is an inequality of power and where touching is prohibited. It's no wonder that love in the therapeutic relationship has been described as a double-edged sword. Since the earliest days of psycho-analytic-style therapies, pioneer therapists like Sigmund Freud recognised that transference has both a healing side and a dark, potentially problematic side.

The healing side of transference is that it keeps therapy focused on the patient and creates the opportunity for a 'corrective experience' to be played out in a safe place. For example: if, like me, your faultlines were formed by your father's abandonment, you may fantasise that your male therapist embodies the qualities you always craved but never knew. This makes him seem like everything you ever wanted – your dream dad made flesh and blood.

Getting a taste of feeling loved and accepted by a dad-like figure through experiencing a therapist's care can be deeply healing and informative. By feeling first-hand something of what father love might have felt like, you get to bask in it; at other times, you can grieve what you never had rather than remain trapped, crying for the moon. No longer are you wandering the Lovelands so aimlessly, yearning after an unknown fantasy.

To a person who has always longed for that kind of deep connection with another, but has never known how to create it, the new experience of being unconditionally accepted can feel like water in the desert, life where there was only the prospect of loneliness in the badlands. It's a powerful way to learn about love.

By experiencing acceptance and validation by a therapist you also begin to understand how to give that quality of emotional presence and caring to yourself and others. When you experience a higher quality of love than you previously knew about, it raises your inner standards and expectations for the future.

Knowing what's possible, and that you are worthy of love, opens the door to more fulfilling relationships and signposts the way out of repeatedly choosing the wrong partners.

I fell in love with Josh's soul as I perceived it because, with all my pain and faultlines on display, Josh liked me and respected me. In fact, he liked me all the more for owning my flaws and expressing my humanity. I was reborn a person with self-respect largely because he showed it to me. I began to see myself as worthy in a way I actually believed.

Now to the dark side. Unfortunately, transference creates the perfect conditions for a giant unrequitable crush. Such a crush can make it difficult to find a real-world love that can ever match up to the fantasy. Kind of like a drug, a fantasy love might seem to hold the promise of a fabulous high and an escape from pain; but it cannot resolve an old longing for love defined by a stubbornly held fantasy of what could be if only *everything* was different.

Twenty-four-year-old Lira, a Canadian woman, and sixty-three-year-old Australian Bruce came to my office with dangerously different objectives. She wanted commitment, he wanted never to see her again.

They'd met as community development workers on a project in Cambodia and began an undercover relationship amongst a close circle of coworkers. Lira said they had wanted to keep things quiet to avoid gossip. Bruce said that he was embarrassed by their relationship because of the age difference and that he knew it would never last in the long run.

Lovers who are coworkers have to juggle different roles. Even when they're not extramarital, workplace affairs are frequently complicated. Concealing the relationship, or at least putting it aside during work hours, can often be a source of tension. For Bruce, the relationship began out of loneliness and impulsivity, against his better judgement. He expressed never being fully in it, his gut twisted in guilt by his stark ambivalence towards Lira right from the start. He had never found himself behaving so coldly in a relationship before and he hated himself for it.

Typically he would feel tender and sad, call Lira and tell her he needed her. In the morning he would regret it, know that he had not been true to either of them, that he had nothing in common with her aside from work and loneliness. The couple was stumbling about in Projection Pass, circling around completely different versions of reality and each other. I imagined them covering their ears so as not to hear the painful truths or unwanted yearnings the other tried to express.

Periodically, Bruce would break up with Lira and try to shut her out of his world, but then he'd find her in his bed upon returning home and would let her stay. When he demanded his key back, she turned up on his doorstep, inconsolable, saying she loved him, begging to talk. When he let her in, the cycle of intimacy and rejection began again.

The significant age gap between them was less relevant than the fact he and Lira were at opposite life stages. She wanted a family while his children were long grown, having kids of their own. His children could not accept his relationship with Lira when they finally found out about it. She was younger than all of them but, more than that, they knew their father's heart was not in the relationship and that it was unhealthy and unsustainable.

Bruce's long marriage to their mum had been over for years but the couple had become great friends as grandparents. He enjoyed the freedom to travel, balanced with time with his kids and grandkids in Australia and the US. He didn't want a new wife or a second family. He just wanted out.

All of this he said in front of Lira in our first meeting. I was saddened and astounded by his outright coldness but Lira didn't seem to flinch. I soon understood why. She'd heard it all before. 'I came here so you can tell her and maybe she'll listen to you,' Bruce said to me.

Lira sat silent and fuming inside until it was her turn to speak. Then she eloquently raged at Bruce's ambivalence, at the mixed messages he had given her over their months together, at his unloving actions, at the cruelty of his words.

Her passion was clearly misplaced on a man who did not love her or share her dreams, desires or values. I sniffed faultlines of yearned-for father love because Lira did not feel compelled to take sovereignty of her Lovelands and exit this loveless mess she was in. Lira had low expectations of love. She was willing to take crumbs from a man old enough to be her grandfather, who denied her loving commitment, played with her feelings and pushed her away afterwards.

Lira had become obsessive about getting Bruce to care for her as though it could be achieved through the force of her will. *We become obsessed with what we did not have.*

She would not let go out of pride or even self-preservation when Bruce told her that he didn't love her. She wanted to make it right, become the beloved instead of the shunned girl. She could not, would not, see that Bruce was *not* her safe place to have a corrective experience of being loved.

In psychology we sometimes speak of the distancer/pursuer dynamic in couples, where one partner controls the intimacy levels through their rollercoaster ambivalence. Lira and Bruce were off the scale. Never before had I so hoped a client relationship would end sooner than it did. So much damage was being done.

Eventually Lira did let go, accepting a new overseas posting so that she couldn't visit Bruce anymore. Changing countries felt like the only way she could stop. He remained in Australia and at last the roller-coaster relationship ended.

Months later when we had a follow-up call via Skype, Lira told me she didn't know what she was thinking to obsess over Bruce as she had. Lira had been seeing mirages of pure love in an arid, empty desert of a relationship. Such is the power of projection.

Projection is, to some extent, inevitable in relationships. We can't help but flavour our image of others with our own fantasies and assumptions about them. Holding doggedly to a fantasy when all evidence is telling you to let go, as in Lira's case, is unhealthy, but some fantasies can be great to play with. Fantasy can be a source of erotic pleasure so long as it isn't in control, overshadowing your reality.

My patient Elly was in love with fantasy – in hot, rapturous love with the stories she wrote in her head in bed at night. When she had sex with her husband, Jake, she imagined random snippets of erotic fantasy, editing in images and seductive action in flashes, like storyboarding a screenplay.

The hot scenes her consciousness unfolded were always in the third person, although Elly knew she *was* her characters. When she inhabited and narrated her fantasies, Elly stepped back emotionally and watched her fantasy selves who were free of responsibility for their actions because nobody could get hurt, nobody could judge. Elly could let go and embody lust.

She said the third-person perspective gave her the space to do anything, be anyone, break all the rules and taboos she might otherwise limit even her imagination from touching. Her fantasies were just too un-PC. For her.

Inhabiting her fantasy scenarios was the only way Elly could orgasm. It had always been her way, but now she felt guilty that she didn't think of Jake at all during sex. Even though she found him sexy, the stuff in her head was more of a turn-on than the reality of married life. Despite her erotic imagination – or because of her guilt about it – Elly's marriage became strained, first in the bedroom, then beyond. Confusion and frustration seeped into their daily lives as the couple's erotic connection became loaded with anxiety and Elly started to avoid sex.

So much of sex happens in the mind. Elly eventually realised she'd made a deficit out of a rare and precious treasure. By judging herself and pulling back in guilt and fear rather than sharing her erotic world with Jake, she was robbing them both of her full and authentic self. No wonder their sex life was dead.

When we make a partnership for life, sharing our erotic worlds is ideally part of the deal – for better or worse. If you won't let yourselves do this out of sexual shame, or if you don't feel the desire for your partner that feeds eroticism into your relationship, you'll likely experience ongoing fantasies of something more.

Elly decided to risk letting Jake into her erotic imagination, little by little, sharing her hot narratives with him in intense moments. As it turned out, her fantasies were not too hot for Jake, nor too shameful. Not even close. It was an emotional risk but it paid off for Jake and Elly. Instead of visiting the hot springs of her Lovelands alone, Elly took Jake with her. Jake too began to whisper his erotic thoughts to her, more images than scenarios, less wordy than Elly's imagination, but every bit as exotic to everyday life as her white-hot inner landscapes. They found ways to be more fully *present*, rather than turning away from each other into private fantasies and experiences. Their minds and bodies were now together in a shared part of their Lovelands.

Fantasy can be food for love, or it can be a solitary path of constant yearning, of living your pleasure alone in your head because your reality doesn't match up. I got trapped for some time, enchanted by the fantasy of Josh as 'the perfect one', although I knew little about him in reality. Although I tried hard to push my feelings for Josh from my awareness, the faultlines of lusting for unavailable, unattainable love had me again.

You need to have the courage to take what you've learned from your role model in a therapeutic relationship and go out and create your own real-world relationships. You need to map your way out of Projection Pass if you want to create a full experience of loving. It takes mindfulness, awareness and patience.

~

Have you ever had a powerful ongoing fantasy about someone in your life or a person you didn't even know? What were the qualities you believed they had that you longed for or admired?

It's worth considering these questions because in our fantasies we reveal to ourselves the qualities, the feelings, the things we most desire. Recognising the qualities we find so compelling in another person can show us what we long to develop in ourselves. I didn't yet realise that the wisdom, awareness, fun, strength and unbounded loving I sought in a partner accurately reflected what I longed to bring out in myself.

When we yearn so badly to find a partner, to feel that whole, special connection with another person, it's difficult to slow down and wait for the right person. We may take a scattergun approach to the search for love rather than being patient, narrowing the field and focusing on making a good choice for the long term.

I should know. I would wait no longer for love, and my hastiness and impatience got me into all sorts of trouble.

10

FOMO LOVE

Sex without love is as hollow and ridiculous as love without sex.

I was still in the chrysalis stage of therapy when Will came along. It was much too soon after Pete for me to jump into another relationship. Will and I were completely wrong for each other but I didn't want to be alone and, I'm sad to say, it still felt normal to accept so much less from a relationship than I actually desired.

Twenty-plus years of programming are not quickly undone and change is not always accomplished on the first try. I saw so many qualities in Josh that I longed for in a man, but I didn't believe I could find someone as desirable as he was because I'd never met anyone like him. Sad, I know. Inaccurate and sad. Despite reaping the rewards of greater happiness and self-acceptance, romantic relationships were still an area in which I had much to learn.

Will was not long out of a divorce followed by a chaotic rebound relationship. He was starting again in Melbourne and needed a place to live. I had a room to rent and we fell into a life together.

Housemates is all we ever should have been. I found him brittle and moody, even in the beginning. It was never passionate between us; it was just friendly and homely because when we met we were both lonely and wanted to share a life with someone. We could have been friends, for a while. If we hadn't been living in the same flat we wouldn't have lasted more than a couple of dates.

He wasn't my kind and I knew it. I wasn't his kind either. I rationalised this was a good thing because I'd been so bad at relationships in the past that I needed to choose differently even if this meant going against my usual points of attraction in a person. I wanted to be in emotional control of myself now, rather than feeling my heart was once again at the mercy of some charismatic, attractive but ultimately emotionally unavailable man.

An accountant, Will was the opposite of the rockstar types I usually dated. So instead of looking for someone who embodied an erotic charge for me, I went to the other end of the spectrum, hoping to sidestep future pain by avoiding anyone I felt dangerously attracted to. Besides,

I was determined to create a new life after acting and choosing a relationship with someone who had nothing to do with the industry seemed smart.

When I started my psychology degree I became single-minded about becoming a psychologist and walking in the shoes of my therapist idol. I talked about human potential and relationship dynamics ad nauseam and I studied with ferocity, stopping only to teach yoga classes and attend therapy. I felt strong, alive and purposeful at last. I raved about my passions to Will and my enthusiasm captured his interest. He was needy then and I was redefining myself as a 'helper' so we fitted together very well in that way.

Will helped me in some practical ways I wasn't so good at. He helped me settle down from my clubbing days into a more regular life, something for which I am grateful to him to this day. He moved through his life with pattern and steadiness, which was balancing because I tended to be emotion-led and spontaneous.

However, Will had faultlines too and I would discover that his pain could be heavy, cold and relentless for him and for me. I told myself it didn't matter that there was little erotic charge between us because, with awareness of how my past had led me to be attracted to difficult men, I'd put sex on the back burner for a while.

I had decided somewhere inside me that desire was my downfall; but looking back, I see that at various times it was naivety, impulsivity, impatience or fear, rather than desire, that led me up the wrong relationship paths. Impatience and fear were both huge factors in wanting to be with Will because after the long, heartbreaking demise of the relationship with Pete, I was afraid of never finding 'the one' and always being alone. Josh, understandably, didn't seem too impressed with my FOMO (Fear Of Missing Out) rationale for getting together with Will, but Josh wasn't there to keep me warm at night.

I know *now* that effective change does not come from just choosing – then doggedly continuing to choose – against your instincts. I eventually learned that it is vital to clarify the qualities that are most important to you in a partner so you're not completely without a map when finding the kind of person who will make you happiest. At the same time, you want to be open-minded that *your* kind can come in an unexpected package, but be a delight to unwrap. While holding your 'shopping list' in mind, it's important to also remember your faultlines, your areas of neediness and vulnerability, and manage yourself safely around them.

Balance the qualities you're attracted to with the characteristics in a partner that work best when combined with your strengths and vulnerabilities. Don't leave reasonable safety standards off your wishlist, but neither should you sell out desire for safety. It won't work, not in the long term. Most people need some of both or it's only a matter of time before unhappiness, or worse, grows from denying desire.

Will and I built a cosy coexistence but gradually, for the first time in my life, I stopped caring about sex almost entirely. I was wandering the Mirages, telling myself I could see the possibility of a passionate relationship, like a gorgeous hot spring shimmering just ahead of us in the Lovelands. But Will and I never seemed to get there. Each time I convinced myself that we could, we would, that this was *as good as it gets* for me, something inside me said, 'No, it isn't' and the mirage faded away.

I realise *now* that I was repressing big erotic feelings for Josh, thereby numbing myself out, but I was doing it so effectively that I wasn't consciously aware of what is now so screamingly obvious. You see, to 'own' my adult sexual attraction to Josh would have screwed up my imagined perfect platonic love between us that allowed me to feel like a treasured, special daughter for the first time in my life.

I shared a great deal about therapy with Will, returning home excited by new insights, bright-eyed and gushing with intense admiration for Josh. Rather than seeing it as a threat to our relationship, to his credit Will seemed to be almost as fascinated as I was.

Our after-therapy discussions helped us understand how our families had shaped the way we were in the world, and gave us new ways to handle our extended family dynamics; my therapy sessions were deeply supportive to both of us in this practical way. But my secret shame and confusion about my slightly obsessive feelings for Josh did not help my relationship with Will.

These days, as a couple therapist, I tell my patients that there is no such thing as a good secret from your partner aside from perhaps a surprise gift. Apart from that, if you need to keep it a secret there's probably some shame or fear that's not healthy for either of you attached to stuff you hide. A bit of mystique is sexy in a relationship, but secrets are emotionally dangerous.

I was absolutely ashamed of my erotic fantasies about Josh and also of my lack of erotic feelings for Will. I didn't want to face rejection from Josh by telling him how I felt about him. Similarly, I didn't want to lose the cosy life I had made with Will by facing up to our sexual deficits. So I loved Will in the ways that were authentic for me – emotional caring, friendship, sharing a comfy home and helping him navigate his faultlines. I kept the erotic stuff a shameful secret, almost from myself too.

I went through a few years – yes, *years* – where I decided that sex was pretty base animal stuff and I aspired to a higher moral ground. The idea first came from my devotion to yoga and spiritual practice – I wanted to live as a pure spirit as much as possible and fantasised about relegating my 'basic urges' as embarrassing asides to daily life. This would have been great if I were single, a nun, and living in a yoga ashram devoting myself to religion; but it was a bit impractical for my life with a partner. I can see now that it was also downright unfair.

I see now that my conviction that sex was low and 'un-spiritual', which is completely inaccurate for me, served me in two big ways. It both justified avoiding sex with Will *and* justified having all my erotic feelings centred around someone (Josh) who was completely unavailable. I was still following the same old pattern of falling for the unavailable man – even in therapy!

My relationship with Will bumbled along only because we had other priorities. Like me, he had decided to study for a career that held more meaning for him than accounting. Occasionally he would be angry with me about the infrequency of sex in our relationship and his demands would put me off even more. He didn't know how to be seductive and masculine in the ways I craved. Will had his good qualities but we were not the right fit and others saw this very clearly. I chose not to listen, hoping the mirage of a perfect relationship wouldn't elude us forever, but deep inside I knew the others were right. We could have given up on each other many times, but we had a home and stability. I was Will's unpaid, full-time live-in therapist and he was my melancholy but ever-present friend. I was determined to help him with his sadness, to heal him and make him happy. Looking back, I can see how crazy this was because his faultlines were not about me.

They came before me and they would continue to exist regardless of anything I said or did until he was ready to heal them himself.

By the time I truly understood how much more there was to experience in a relationship, I was married to Will. I married him out of fear of starting again from scratch because, more than anything in the world, I wanted a family and so did he. I wasn't going to take the chance of waiting too long for a fantasy and miss the boat. I knew in my soul it was foolhardy to marry without desire, but when the choice between 'marry Will now' or 'start again' lay before me, it was just too awful to contemplate starting again.

So many people marry out of FOMO, and I think most of them know it but they just don't want to admit it in case they miss the marriage-and-kids boat. It's common as a couple therapist to hear people in a private moment confide that they share no great love story of passion with their partner. They stayed together because when the time came to decide whether they were life partners or not they chose the devil they knew, despite serious misgivings and a dearth of passionate feelings. The other common scenario of passionless marriage remains the traditional classic – getting pregnant and feeling like the pregnancy made the decision for them.

I had unconsciously decided long ago that there were princesses who knew unconditional father love in their

DNA and then there were the non-princesses who didn't. I was a non-princess, unloved by my own father. Since Will had chosen me, a known non-princess, as a life partner, I felt I would be a fool not to accept. If I had waited until my self-esteem had recovered more, until I had rebuilt myself and found my way through my personal desert, I could have seen clearly that my mirage-like marriage to Will was always going to fall apart.

That being said, there is usually some good in every bad decision. Every relationship teaches us a great deal about ourselves and about love. There are few universally 'right' answers in love; the challenge is choosing the best answer for your body, mind and soul. Sometimes you must follow a path to learn more about your identity, your wants and to find the courage of your desires. The wrong path might just be the right path *at the time*. No regrets.

~

My friend Jack was gay and afraid of his sexuality. He was attractive, with thick, glossy shoulder-length hair, gold earrings, brown skin and a whole lot of George Michael sexy going on. I went to yoga class with him for a couple of years, but when he stopped attending we lost touch.

I was surprised when, a few years later, he and his new wife, Katie, walked into my yoga centre. Katie was withdrawn, kind, passive and strikingly overweight. She was Jack's ever-present one, his confidante in all things – except sex.

Katie didn't stay for class and afterwards Jack and I had coffee in the cafe downstairs. Katie and Jack had been best friends since primary school and they clearly loved one another. There was no sexual chemistry whatsoever between them – he told me this openly. Not even a glimmer. But this hadn't stopped him from proposing to her at twenty-six, after dating for ten years and being friends for almost twenty.

He said he was afraid of missing out on having kids and, most of all, a 'normal' life. He told me he chose to be with Katie because she wanted the same things he did and she loved him completely. He believed his heart would always be safe with her.

I wondered how they would have those kids without having sex, but what could I say? I didn't need to play therapist to him and he didn't want me to. We both knew he was following a path that was likely to end in tears, and plenty of them.

I don't know how things worked out for them, or didn't. Fear is strong but love is stronger. More than that, I am convinced that there is not always *one* right answer and that every person can declare sovereignty over themselves and their Lovelands without the approval of any other, friend or therapist. It can be agonising to watch another's decisions but there's a fine line between supportive reflection and distancing criticism.

Each of us can elect to listen to fear and embrace the devil we know – it's our prerogative. Or we can choose not to settle for a relationship we sense isn't right for us. It's all just a matter of discovering your truth, then deciding what you want to do with that powerful wisdom.

There are mirages in the Lovelands; sometimes things are not what they seem. Fears that look so terrible may be nothing but shadows or we may not be as trapped or lost as we think we are. Sometimes we just have to keep putting one foot in front of the other until things become clearer.

Whatever you choose, two things:

1. You can change your mind.

2. No regrets.

11

MOTHER LOVE

Motherhood: All love begins and ends there.

ROBERT BROWNING

I wanted to have a child and Will wanted one too, although unfortunately we were struggling to find much fun or passion as a couple. I still questioned whether I could ever experience the kind of love, with Will or with anyone else, that approximated my dream love. I was fairly convinced that I couldn't because it just was not my karma, not this life, because I had married the way I did. I felt resigned, melancholy sometimes, yet *almost* at peace because I understood myself at last, and I wanted a baby very badly.

I finished therapy a few months before the baby was due. In our last session in a decade of sessions, Josh joked that I would forget about him soon. Part of me felt strong and thrilled and free as I walked away from being the client for the last time, and part of me was incredibly sad. Josh said that a part of him wished he could continue beside me, but he was very happy and proud to know how far we had come, how much we had seen together and, most of all, that I no longer needed him. He also said that he would miss me very much.

Four months later I became mother to my baby boy who arrived from the Sea of Bliss Dreams and immediately took full sovereignty of my heart. Motherhood changed everything about who I was because now I had somebody else who was entirely my responsibility, someone more important to me than me. My primary focus became the fulfilment of the bliss dream for my little one. More than anything else, I wanted his life to be free of the primal shame of abandonment and feeling not good enough; feelings that had come dangerously close to trapping me in the badlands.

My kid was, and is, surrounded by a powerful love on all sides. I had learned so much from what I didn't have as a child and I wanted nothing more than for my son to benefit from my wisdom and experience. I was at a place where, finally, all the years of work on myself as a person and a professional were showing rewards and I had the baby of my dreams. Life would have been perfect but for the marriage Will and I had made. It satisfied neither of us.

It's at times of adjustment, such as new parenthood, that a couple either turns towards each other in love and understanding to cope as a team, or turns away from one another into their own worlds to lick their wounds solo. We inadvertently chose the latter. I knew it was happening, even at the time, but with a wakeful child and a connection that was wearing too thin, I felt unable to do better. Will seemed to resent the lack of erotic connection even more than before, now that my emotional support for him also waned.

When I had the baby I no longer had the energy or the desire to focus on Will. I wanted Will to take care of *me* while I focused on our child. It was not an adjustment we were able to make. I was engrossed in my child because having a baby was the single most miraculous event of my life. Watching him grow as a person, to this day, fascinates me. It's a feat, mothering – on the one hand feeling as though this other being is a part of you, an extension of your own self; then gradually having to allow more space as they grow and stretch themselves. Watching my baby explore away from me was like letting my heart jump out of my chest, raw, to stumble about in front of me.

The love affair with my child's soul is unyielding and untouchable to any other force because it *is* elemental life force. It's pure love that can change form but can never die. I had never known a feeling like it and I cannot commend it more highly as an experience that reaches beyond one life, beyond all death, beyond all other forces – a force to be experienced. Loving my child teaches me that love is utterly undefeatable. No matter what happens, love is there. The love for my child gave me enormous strength because I was no longer so needy within myself; yet it made me more vulnerable because I felt tied to my little one with all my heart, my existence seeming to hang on his wellbeing.

As I watch him grow I'm constantly surprised and in awe of life. He's another window through which I appreciate everything, through which I have experienced true selflessness for the first time. When I grasped that meaning in life for me was in loving this other being and supporting his wellbeing, I understood the reality of our interconnectedness with others like I never had before.

I had grown up with an idea of independence and individuality being so very important, an idea of breaking away from the crowd being so desirable. The idea of need-ing others, although secretly wished for, was often pushed aside as weak and foolish. Now I understood interdepend-ence as an inescapable human reality and family as the most fundamental of needs. I know it sounds odd that it took having my own baby to discover how strong the desire for family was in me but, with an absent dad, a crazy stepfather and a tenuous marriage, I had given up on family as a viable idea until I became a parent. I thrived on being with my child always, on providing him with secure attachment, unlike the loss and confusion I had felt as my mother struggled to care for me and work full-time throughout my childhood. He and I were never apart for more than a couple of hours in a row for years, because that's how it worked for us.

Cultivating a deep and secure attachment style in a child takes consistent presence while also allowing the child to venture and learn. I respect the many different ways parents can parent and I hasten to say that there is no 'one size fits all' when it comes to raising healthy kids. There is, however, a fact that holds true for all humans, which is influenced by the parenting we receive at the early stages of development: a secure attachment style in close relationships is associated with better mental health and wellbeing across the lifespan. This being said, it's never too late to map your Lovelands, understand what you missed out on and choose your own path to where you want to go.

One of my life's greatest pleasures is watching my child's passions, empathy and intelligence evolve and emerge. Although children's development is constant, it isn't always visible or at a steady rate. Young beings tend to percolate for a while, then boil over into a leap forward every so often, as a pattern. Much private growth happens during seemingly quiet times, then a whole lot of newness explodes into the public domain. To me, the surprises are awe inspiring.

I would be lying if I didn't also confess that motherhood brings its tensions and stresses, the greatest one for many business and creative types being the 'focus-suck' away from the art or vocation that once monopolised our minds, hearts and days. Mothering is intensely creative, yet also filled with a fair share of drudge work, especially when kids are very young. There can be a real ache to find more time to escape into the flow of solo passions again instead of being relentlessly focused on the needs of another. I certainly experienced a sense of loss around my writing time that had been my major focus for many years, especially those years leading up to the pregnancy when I had been immersed in writing my PhD.

I've heard it said that parenting is an exercise in guilt-management because it involves constantly balancing your own needs with the infinite needs of dependent little ones. While it's guilt-inducing to admit that sometimes I craved a retreat into writing when my child was young, it wouldn't be fair to pretend the transition to creating a family was completely joyous and tension free. Finding a balance between being a mother and keeping some of the self you were before is important for sanity. I do believe that getting 'me time' lets you relax into being a better mum because you've had a creative outlet of your own and released some of your creative tension, feeling flow instead of frustration. Like in all relationships, you need to fill up your tank so you've got more to give.

Although I sometimes wondered where I'd ever find the time to focus on myself again in motherhood, it has actually been readily recoupable. In the bigger picture, I've realised that, as author Gretchen Rubin astutely observed, the days of motherhood can feel very long but the years smash past at speed. At risk of sounding like an old lady, I feel compelled to remark how quickly it seems that a baby suddenly arrives at the verge of manhood or womanhood and you're thinking, 'Where the hell did those years go?' We have to remember how short those childhood years are and focus on using them to equip kids with optimism, emotional freedom, healthy ways of coping with the world, an experiential understanding of love and kindness.

Knowing love, and subsequently knowing how to give love to ourselves and to others, begins in childhood. Children need conscious support and help to develop and strengthen empathy in relationships. Kids need support to learn how to recognise the strengths and passions they discover in themselves, and how to enjoy flow and immersion in life. They need to learn that love involves giving your attention, your full presence, freely to another, something a child can only comprehend through receiving it. Most of all, kids need to appreciate kindness and respect for themselves and others by being given it fully and completely, and knowing that there is no other pathway to peace and happiness than a life where love is the top priority.

Loving others deeply is one of the great loves that creates a passionate existence. There is always a way to give love and there is always a child who needs mother love in some capacity.

I met Lily when she was battling the final stages of terminal illness. She wanted a place to reflect and organise her thoughts with someone who wasn't going to panic when she spoke about the practical end-of-life stuff she wanted to express.

Lily was a highly organised, affectionate mother of multiple foster children over twenty years. Disease had stolen biological motherhood from her but it had not stolen her mother-spirit. Even as she became physically frail, her inner power shone through in her mothering of her adopted daughter. Mary was the last child she'd fostered some years before, a girl with no parents to return to.

Lily endured two years of gut-wrenching palliative medical treatments to be present for her daughter for as long as she could. Mary was her reason to live when she wanted to die and end the pain. Mary was her joy and legacy and, fed by Lily's joy, Mary thrived, won awards for her talents and became part of a strong community. Lily openly and lovingly did all she could to prepare the girl and those around her, especially Mary's adoptive father, Michael, Lily's husband of twenty-two years, for life after her. Although she was often in pain herself, in her last few months Lily led her friends and family through the Plains of Uncertainty, picking them up when they stumbled over fear. She helped them map the landmarks and faultlines to look out for on their return journey. She knew that she wouldn't continue with them through the Lovelands for much longer, but she hoped to impart as much of her hard-won knowledge of the terrain as she could before her journey ended.

When Lily died at forty-seven, she left detailed supportive wisdom in journals for Mary to turn to in the years to come. She had created an informed, involved and ready community of friends and professionals around her family and put in place all she could to help Mary and Michael through their grief. Still, she told me, she sometimes felt guilty that she was going, that she could not stay, as if somehow it was her fault. Mary didn't need another loss, she said.

We reflected on how much Mary had gained, and everything that she would always have – a detailed, intricate map of the Lovelands drawn by hand with loving care, just for her. Without Lily and Michael she may never have known the experience of love that is now hers forever. To this day, even when times are tough, Mary shines with strength and confidence, just like her mum did.

12

SELF-LOVE

Love is the essential reality and our purpose on earth. To be consciously aware of it, to experience love in ourselves and others, is the meaning of life. Meaning does not lie in things. Meaning lies in us.

MARIANNE WILLIAMSON

As we explored in the previous chapter, to give love to others is our greatest gift, but another of the great and vital loves of our lives is self-compassion. Finding your self-compassion is like discovering a lake in the heart of your Lovelands with lotus flowers floating near its shores. The lotus comes from the mud but blooms into great beauty, symbolising how we too can flourish from dark or messy beginnings. The Lake of Self-Compassion is a place of replenishment and healing; it is vast enough for all of us to find if we're willing to look.

Love in the form of self-compassion gives us peace, a home inside ourselves that nothing can take away. It's as if in the core of you a pilot light roars to life when you turn up the gas with passionate goals, self-care, joy, giving and flow. You've felt it surge – it's your energy, it's the divine spark in you, the essential life force that animates you. It's love and compassion for your being – the same love you can share with others.

When I work as a therapist with people who are suffering, when I get down digging in the pain of their constellation of symptoms and stumble with them over their faultlines, I usually discover that their spark of self-love and aliveness is somehow obscured. Their tough little pilot light is still there, but it might be sputtering, smothered, starving for air. The job is usually to negotiate the pathways, sometimes long and complex, to get that spark glowing and firing up more often, more fully.

Self-love, which is essentially self-compassion, is in us regardless of how many times we screw up. While we're alive it's in us, because love is the energy of life. When you're ready, you discover that *you* were always waiting for you with self-love and compassion.

The best vantage point for a first glimpse of the Lake of Self-Compassion is from Mindfulness Mountain. Self-compassion becomes more possible when you start to identify with yourself as more than just your thoughts and feelings in any given moment; when you experience *being* yourself without judging yourself.

I finally arrived at a place of self-love on an ordinary day with no fanfare. I found myself walking down to the lake with only myself to greet me, aware that something had shifted in the way I saw myself. It suddenly dawned on me so clearly that to continue to be so hard on myself, deny myself and talk down to myself out of habit would never help anyone.

Let's be clear that when I say 'self-love' I'm not talking about vanity or narcissism. Narcissistic love is the need to be seen as special in order to feel safe and survive. It's natural and normal to have that need when we are children. However, a mature love is a whole-hearted commitment to know, experience and contribute as deeply as possible to the growth of someone or something and to help them become as fully joyful and realised as they can be. Self-love is that commitment to yourself, as well as to others. The difficult thing about re-connecting with self-love can be that when it is obscured by pain, the road back is not always simple to find.

To make it harder, there are a lot of mixed messages out there about 'loving yourself', which kept me confused for years. Self-love as open pride in yourself is generally not seen as a good move socially, which makes the popular self-help phrase, 'You've got to love yourself before you can love anyone else' rather difficult to accommodate. Then there are all the other platitudes, such as: 'Love is all you need.' 'Love is the drug.' 'God is love.'

Most cultures are a bit obsessed with love, and why not? Love is a need that is evident on brain scans, lighting up the most primitive part of our brain, the part that relates to our survival needs. It's because we *need* love that it is longed for, dreamed about, misunderstood, discussed constantly online and off, sometimes sold out cheap or completely mislabelled. Love is the most widely aspired-to feeling of all human emotions and the loss of love can provoke some of our greatest pain, activating the worst in us, as well as the best.

For people with low self-esteem, self-love is a particularly difficult concept to grasp and make use of. I remember getting so angered by platitudes about how I needed to love myself in order to love others fully. I would think, 'Well, how the hell do I make that happen when I just don't feel it?' I wondered if it meant I could never create a good relationship if I wasn't able to somehow magically like myself more.

Later I realised that it's getting to a place of calm and awareness of the faultlines that matters in self-compassion, not some surreal, cheesy, smiley feeling of self-satisfaction. I also realised that we learn to know ourselves, understand ourselves, care for ourselves and accept ourselves better through relationships with others, rather than in isolation. We are not at our best in solitude, at least not for long. We are beings of relationship and interconnection. We are tribal.

Love gets so dragged through fairytales, fantasy, projection and technology that we can lose sight of what it really is. In the age of internet porn and super-fast hook-ups, love and sex get pretty mangled and a cold hard device doesn't always facilitate transmission of the reverence and respect that help people flourish and relationships grow.

Love depends on mindfulness to some extent because we don't feel deeply loved without perceiving some presence of mind and heart from another, or from ourselves. We desperately need more education around loving well, particularly around treating ourselves lovingly as a way of life. Different human problems naturally require different treatment regimes, different therapies; but to me, there's no cure in which loving, compassionate caring, perhaps from another, but always from ourselves, is not a vital, active ingredient. Let's get practical about self-love with my best tips for developing the life skill of self-compassion:

Mindfulness

Just as love flows through attending deeply to another, self-love or self-compassion is strengthened through extending mindful attention to our inner world rather than taking it for granted. By noticing what's happening inside us in the moment, we can observe that some thoughts support us and some hurt us. We care for ourselves deeply by making choices about the thoughts and feelings we want to buy into. We build resilience by learning to expand around thoughts and feelings and calmly exist *with* them rather than avoiding them or fusing with them.

Peak experiences

We can embody self-love and compassion through giving ourselves permission to discover and follow our passions and find our way into the state that psychologist Abraham Maslow called 'peak experience'. A peak experience is just like the flow state or our 'zone of genius' as it involves utter absorption. Time melts away and there is nothing but *being* in the experience of each moment as it comes and goes. In flow or a peak experience, we are in communion with our passion – we are in a space of *being* love.

Author Joan Borysenko wrote that in experiencing flow, colours seem more vibrant, sounds richer. Textures can come alive. In flow, we get behind words and fantasies about love. We simply *abide* in what or who we love. When we experience ourselves in this kind of love, we know ourselves better, we like ourselves better.

Self-forgiveness

Forgiveness is a vital part of clearing the dross and turning up the gas on self-love and compassion. We've all made mistakes and there is no point in running from them if they want your attention. Just say to unhelpful thoughts, 'Hello, old friend. What are you trying to teach me or warn me about today? I have other things I must focus on right now.'

Emotional responsibility

We can take notice of how we feel and take responsibility for our emotional responses rather than reacting or blaming others for our feelings and our struggles. Emotional responsibility means not lashing out in rage or frustration at others. It means cultivating the patience to reflect on inner assumptions and become aware of prejudices rather than automatically letting our animal-brain rule our behaviour and our words. Emotional responsibility *responds* mindfully rather than *reacts* thoughtlessly. Responding mindfully means not getting caught up in a spiral of reactivity and subsequent guilt and regrets.

Presence

The need for love is the need for healthy, deep attentiveness to our soul and other souls. When children plead for attention they are pleading to feel loved and connected to another by playing, by learning, and by just being together, focused together. It's the same in adults although it looks a bit different. Consistently unattended requests for loving presence can painfully twist into destructive behaviour, shame and withdrawal; or into internalising feelings of just not mattering that much to anyone. Love asks us to have a generosity of spirit towards others, to trust that the energy of love is infinite. We won't run out if we give a little extra.

Self-acceptance

As I began to understand myself better, I found that developing self-esteem was less onerous and unattainable than I had imagined it to be. It actually wasn't as big a deal to think kindly of myself. Really, the key was catching myself when I was being mean to myself – judging, regretting, comparing or complaining about myself in my thoughts – then stopping. I didn't have to kiss myself or say 'I love you' in the mirror ten times a day. I just had to stop being so mean to me.

Maybe, ultimately, there *are* things about you that you can never like, never embrace; but so what. We can't change the past but we can face our demons, anger and regret and say, 'You're here, you're not going anywhere soon, you're not pretty, I get that. Now let's move on.'

Check your self-talk regularly. Thoughts are not facts. Many are nonsense. Fact.

Self-trust

One of my greatest lessons of therapy was that being a mature person means no longer needing to look to others for the answers in life, but to internally fulfil my searchings and needs more effectively and be my own guide. It was a new gift to be able to ask myself if something made me happy, or was just an expectation or an outdated automatic default, and then give myself a genuine answer. The most important question I learned to ask myself was: 'Is what I am about to say or do likely to be helpful?'

In other words, before reacting, to reflect on the likely consequences for myself and others. I learned to question patterns that were previously defaults and consider my motivations more carefully. I developed the courage and desire to know myself and my capacities more fully, and to see how well I could do if I really tried to achieve my goals and sought to finish things and not give up, putting in the hard work.

Creating better experiences through being mindful, then noting my successes with basic kindness rather than cutting judgement were subtle shifts but hugely consequential. I was able to cultivate genuine trust in my ability to make good choices based on my values, even under pressure, and this fed back into getting it right *for me* more often and subsequently liking myself more.

'Being' time

By taking time to *be* – in meditation, in contemplation – we can give ourselves 'the time of day', give ourselves the loving presence that is our gift to give by listening to our thoughts and sorting the helpful from the unhelpful, supporting ourselves at that deepest level through awareness.

'Being' time can evolve into a pervasive mindfulness in daily life.

'Doing' time

Balance reflection with action. Keep finding ways to light yourself up every day so that you're in the flow of your essence – which is love – because love is the driving force of life and the glue that makes the connections between everything living. Actively give it, breathe it out, and let the return flow look after itself.

Suffering is inevitable no matter how wise we may become, no matter how hard we may try to play it safe. So much is unknown to us. Ahead of us always are Plains of Uncertainty, mirages and dangerous precipices. But no matter where you find yourself in the Lovelands, self-compassion will help you out.

13

—

DANGEROUS LOVE

She had to learn how not to let her eyes be bewildered by manifestations, and thereby learn to treat appearances as signs and codes of the interior.

BEN OKRI

Our faultlines can lead us dangerously astray. We don't always recognise them cracking open a new area of our Lovelands. They can run underground for a long way, suddenly emerging in a distant part of the landscape.

Mount Danger, an active volcano, pushes up from the earth where the Mirages meet the vast, windswept Plains of Uncertainty. If you have a map – meaning you know something of your vulnerabilities and understand what activates them – you have a choice when you see Mount Danger rising ahead of you. You can detour or forge on, regardless of the consequences.

Mark and Lisele came to me in pieces in the aftermath of infidelity. Lisele had fallen hard for a coworker in the hospital where she worked, and during a conference when he'd come to her room, she hadn't refused him. She swore they hadn't had sex but had kissed and spent the night together. Now Lisele was confused about what she wanted and utterly ashamed. She said she felt like a bad cliché, a character from *The Bold and the Beautiful*, torn between love for Ridge and desire for Thorn.

Mark was devastated. He couldn't understand why it had happened when he and Lisele had so much to lose – a family, a home, a marriage. Lisele maintained that Mark was over-reacting as she hadn't actually cheated on him, which sent Mark into a tailspin. They couldn't even agree on something as basic as what constituted infidelity in their relationship. Did the definition start and end with sex? What *kind* of sex? With a kiss? Or with spending a night in a hotel room engaged in intimate conversation?

What about for you? Does infidelity start with texts and phone calls you don't happen to mention? Does it include secret erotic fantasies about others and, if so, as Lisele angrily asked Mark, is pornography included, or doesn't it count if you don't know the people? You decide. It's a difficult discussion but one worth having.

There are many reasons people seek love, sex, pleasure or intimacy outside their relationship, but often they're not cognisant of the reasons, only of compelling desire. When we yearn for a third 'other' it is ourselves we need to tune into before we set out for Mount Danger's smoking summit. In fantasising, we're usually looking for something we feel we've lost or never had that feels vital to us; this is often what the other person represents to us. Sometimes they represent something of who we wish we were in ourselves, as though a union with them might somehow give us a transfusion of their sexiness, power or youth.

There are some qualities we yearn for so strongly that we're prepared to risk everything to feel them. They're not small feelings – to risk so much the stakes *must* be high. We're usually searching for confirmation that we are still alive in some way, pushing aside other options for feeling more potent and erotically charged. After all, many other options just don't look as stimulating to the imagination as the opportunity to pursue fantasy sex, although they may be relationship-saving. Ultimately, the choice is yours. What do you really hope to gain? More specifically, what are you willing to lose?

Recovering from any betrayal of trust is slow and painstaking and the more intimate the betrayal, the rawer the pain, shame, rage and hurt that follows. It takes consistent intense focus, patience and commitment to create a new post-affair relationship if a couple still wants to be together. Many don't make it out of the seared earth of the post-affair landscape and head off in different directions.

Lisele marvelled that as time went by, her attraction to her coworker seemed unlikely and odd, yet it had been so compelling at the time. She came to understand that her affair was a run for freedom, youth, potency and feeling alive – snatching an opportunity to feel hot, passionately loved and lusted for, in an otherwise numbed-out existence. It is usual to find that at the absolute core, infidelity frequently has less to do with any lover's deficits or attributes and more to do with an unacknowledged inner self that's been silently screaming for *something* for a long time.

That's why understanding the personal 'why' of an affair is so important, whether a couple stays together or moves apart in its aftermath. If you've had an affair you need to acknowledge why you ended up chasing your desires and yearnings in such a dramatic, secretive and damaging way. There are many ways to feel alive, to take big risks, to grow, to have sex, to leave – so why did you choose that way?

For the betrayed partner – you must ask yourself not only whether you want to eventually move past the pain of betrayal and stay, but whether you really think you can. Little can be decided in the searing pain of the immediate aftermath of discovering infidelity. You must both get back from the edge of the volcano and give yourselves time to adjust to the new relationship landscape before either of you make any hasty decisions.

Understand that you are each dealing with very different constellations of emotion, grief and pain.

Betrayal can be felt as a deep trauma. Shame and guilt can feel paralysing.

Make your way to the Lake of Self-Compassion as often as you can. After the burning of the old, inevitably come the shoots of new life. Give it time, give the new reality plenty of the waters of compassion and let the smoke clear so that you can find your way off the steep slopes of Mount Danger, be it together or alone.

~

I saw the faultlines emerge unexpectedly a long way off and the smoking mountain rising on the horizon. I held the map of awareness and knowledge, but I was intrigued. I decided to go with the danger.

I *could* handle having a real-life working relationship with my ex-therapist – or so I told myself when Josh suddenly called my office to talk about a referral and suggested a catch-up. It was more than three years after therapy had ended. My stomach flipped, my voice wavered but I kept it together. Just.

I immediately formed high hopes of friendship, of professional and personal sharing, where I could revel in feeling special and connected to him again. I came alive on a whole new level just from hearing his voice, just from knowing he had thought of me and trusted me as a colleague, as an equal. It felt like a pretty amazing endorsement.

I excitedly told Will about the phone call when I got home and he supported me in forming a professional relationship with Josh to help build my practice. He was also impressed that my therapist of so many years was now reaching out to connect with me as a colleague.

Fast forward a couple of months and there was Josh sitting opposite me in a local cafe. He talked to me about his three kids, about his passion for sailing, selling his house, his recent volunteer work as a medical consultant overseas. I listened and ate it all up. It was weird, almost surreal, to talk like friends after years of knowing nothing about his private life. I felt special, trusted, chosen – many of the things I'd yearned to feel with him.

I talked about my child, my work and my world and I enjoyed the bliss of his complete attention, like old times only better, and with food. He said that he wanted to catch up again soon and that it had been great to talk like this. We hugged and I felt momentarily magnetised and thrilled by his warmth. I went to work on a cloud of happiness.

Josh telephoned again, as he said he would, a couple of weeks later. Again we met for coffee and a great chat. It started to become a regular thing – business over coffee every couple of weeks. It was so much fun and I was so proud to enjoy colleague status with Josh. We laughed a lot, confided in each other and became increasingly involved with each other's worlds. Of course I was attracted to Josh but I'd pushed these feelings aside for over a decade. I wasn't going to let them get in the way of a great friendship and real-world connection that I had yearned for with him for so long.

Then one morning after the second cup, Josh announced that he thought it was 'safer' if we didn't meet again. His words were considered and intense. I was surprised and I felt a little panicky that I might be losing him again so soon after reconnecting and imagining that an enduring friendship was underway.

Josh said that his feelings for me were 'dangerous' (what!?), that our meetings had an affair-like quality and we had probably better stop seeing each other. I was stunned into silence, completely gobsmacked, my mind reeling. Everything started to feel a bit blurry, like a TV flashback when the image ripples as the clock is turned back.

Had he been attracted to me all this time? Me, the one who had grown up swimming against a tide of unworthiness, me about whom he knew *everything*? I had gotten his attention in *this* way despite him knowing my every shame and witnessing years of my struggles? I was speechless. I said that I had to go. This kind of attention from Josh had been my fantasy, but real-world feelings were another thing entirely. 'Dangerous' was an understatement. He was my doctor, my mentor, my father-figure? Holy. Shit.

I was mind-blown and confused. I needed to get my thoughts in order over this revelation. Perhaps Josh had expected me to argue against his words but I could barely speak, so no sooner had he said it than he changed his mind. He paid the bill and returned to the table, simply saying that it was my turn to pay for coffee next time. *Next time.*

Outside the cafe it had begun to rain. I was mainly aware of feeling afraid but there was a whole storm of emotions beginning to swirl in my gut. I began to say a hasty goodbye but Josh put his hand out to stop me as I went to walk away.

He softly brushed his hands over my shoulders and down my arms to embrace me, looking into my face with such tenderness. I closed my eyes, right there in the street in broad daylight, and fell into a new, terrifying reality. Confidently, he slid his hands down the sides of my waist and over my hips.

So suddenly it was sexual. Just like that, he crossed the line. The 'father love' immediately went bad, for real. I panicked and took deep breaths as I realised he couldn't be my father-figure anymore. He wasn't my therapist anymore either. In that single tiny moment, on so many levels, so much was irretrievably turned to ashes and scattered to the wind.

Terror of looming loss, confusion about his role in my life combined with unwanted, primal arousal was a nasty, dirty cocktail. He almost held me up while I more than trembled, I really shook. He must have felt it, but he showed no concern. I thought he *should* have been concerned; but no, everything was different. He just looked into my face and smiled.

I jerked away, saying something about the rain and took off up the street running, running in my high-heel boots as if my life depended on it. He was calling out to me and I think he was following me up the street, but I didn't look back. I cried, then I laughed in disbelief, but I didn't look back. Meanwhile, some primal, wild woman part of me I barely recognised was doing all she could to commandeer my ship. She sweated to pursue Josh with her every fibre.

~

It's paradoxical, but making a 'better the devil you know' choice of partner in order to play it safe like Will and I did can actually be a very dangerous decision in the long run. You may find that what you bought was not the benign, flat ground that fear-of-the-unknown tricked you into settling for after all. In actuality, your cosy, erotically disconnected marriage is resting on a dormant but rumbling volcano of resentment and repressed desires. One day a passionless marriage is likely to explode and send a dark cloud over the Lovelands. There are usually a few tremors first that will warn you all is not well, but only if you are willing to pay attention.

The first time Will told me that he wanted to leave was right before our wedding, but he had recanted. He came out with it again when our baby was eighteen months old. He told me in a cold, quiet rage. We had never fully recovered from that revelation but we continued to put one foot in front of the other, neither of us knowing what else to do.

Will gave no specific reasons for why he suddenly wanted to leave, but something had really changed for him. No matter how many times I asked him what was wrong, he would not answer. His wired silence was unnerving. Our life that had been unsatisfying but tolerable suddenly felt intolerable to him without me knowing the reasons for this particular shift. He did eventually give a reason for staying: he had 'nowhere to go'.

From that time on, I had started to imagine life without Will, without the anchor of a marriage that felt so heavy, joyless and irredeemable. It had seemed inevitable we would part. I imagined he would leave me for someone who wanted to be touched by him. I could understand that.

If Will and I had had a strong memory of shared passion and delight to fall back on, now would have been the time to tap into it, reconnect and survive. Yet its absence showed me what a marriage must have to hold joyously at the centre of a family. I learnt how tenuous it is to have kids with a partner if you don't share this strong base. You need a passionate foundation to rely on when the pressure of children comes on. I had foolishly pushed aside this massive shortcoming of our relationship for years, not wanting to admit to it because it would mean selling up and starting again.

My kid was a triumph, my major reason for being, but now that he was three, my own desires were surfacing again, and I guess Will's were too. I fantasised about mothering my kid without the pressure of Will in the background, resenting me. I wanted to laugh again. I wanted to feel passion and joy in a relationship with someone who was right for me and I know that Will felt the same way.

For the last couple of years of our marriage I felt as though Will was actively looking around for an opportunity to move on. One day we were in the park with our child and dog and Will spent a long time talking with one of the local young mums. I had a strange feeling about the interaction and I asked him later if he fancied her. He looked at me shamefacedly and asked me how I knew.

I knew because he looked at her the way he *used* to look at me. To be honest, it bothered me a little bit, but not very much. That's a dangerous place for a relationship to be.

When it's crunch-time in a relationship, everything ultimately hinges on whether a couple turns towards each other to deal with their problems and confusion, or turns away and rejects one another. Your commitment to a shared life, desire for one another, enjoyment of your couple world and the strength of your emotional connectedness all come under a harsh spotlight when pressure is applied to your relationship from outside. Couple research tells us that turning to one another to face challenges as a team is a predictor of marital happiness and longevity. Habitually distancing and turning away from each other to face challenges alone is associated with relationship dissatisfaction and divorce.

Secrecy and developing intense intimacy outside your primary relationship always brings Mount Danger into view. When we feel empty and cannot seem to fill ourselves up from within the relationship, it is almost inevitable that we look to fill ourselves from outside. Therapy can help enormously, and individual therapy can help a person learn how to turn to their partner for intimacy and support. However, long-term individual therapy can be potentially detrimental to a brittle relationship if the therapist inadvertently or actively encourages their patient to turn away from their partner.

I maintain that couple therapy is a far better method to help couples turn to one another because with a good therapist they can be guided and coached in changing their ways and growing *together*. However, it's unlikely that couple therapy can manufacture desire between partners if it was never present from the start. Sometimes you know it was never right. You just have to acknowledge having both made a mistake and having always known it in your hearts.

If you are part of a couple and you want to save your relationship, get couple therapy and get it earlier rather than later. Witness each other's struggles and triumphs in therapy and in life; grow together rather than split off into your own private exploration of love. Understand that you have to keep filling one another and yourselves with love and compassion. Have plenty of gently wicked, joyful fun together and be willing to hear each other's deepest yearnings, rather than setting out for Mount Danger alone in secrecy and shame on a doomed quest.

If you have a great love story together, don't give up easily when times are tough. Life is sometimes tough for everyone, so just give your love your attention again like you did at the start. Love needs our attention to thrive. Love *means* giving each other quality attention and engagement every day. Priority *uno*.

14

LOVE ENDS

Lives fall apart because they're meant to. They need to because they weren't built the right way in the first place. I came to this realisation one day, after many days, weeks, months and years trying to fix the cracks in my foundation.

IYANLA VANZANT

Josh called me frequently after the fateful rainy coffee morning, repeatedly asking to meet again. He said he didn't want to let go, dangerous or not. He wanted to see me.

I refused. I knew that meeting with him now was *absolutely* dangerous. He had been so powerful in my life for so long and now here he was actively pursuing me. How was I going to withstand the emotional force of that?

While I revelled in his attention, I felt simultaneously disgusted by it, and ashamed of not having the courage to confess everything to Will and shut down the contact. My ego loved that Josh was attracted to me, that he now needed me like I had needed him for all those years; but it was wrong for my ex-therapist to pursue me in this way.

I could see the sharp, rocky shores of Broken Heart Beach way off in the distance from the heights of Mount Danger. I didn't want to go to that thankless place, but it was starting to feel like a foregone conclusion. I had to keep fighting.

I deleted Josh's number and threw myself into other aspects of my life with gusto. I screened my calls and stopped picking up my phone, but Josh played constantly on my mind. His attention made me feel attractive and powerful in a way I hadn't experienced for years.

After almost a month of dodging texts and calls I finally picked up a call from a new but persistent unknown number. Of course it was Josh. He was living at his office, he said, in the house by the beach. He told me he had left his wife. I was shocked and I immediately felt like it was somehow my fault because of the feelings he'd expressed. He asked me many times to meet with him. I told him I would not, so he just kept calling and texting.

Over numerous phone calls, Josh told me he had fought with an inner emptiness for a long time for so many reasons, old and new. He had tried to ensure he felt loved and worthy by providing the biggest and the best of everything but focusing on the exterior of his life at the expense of his interior had meant 'killing off' parts of himself to keep going. He felt he had been living with a self-imposed inner 'deadness', a little like I had. He was glad to have woken up to it, yet sad to admit to himself how much time he had wasted not being as emotionally present for his kids as he could have been.

I felt great compassion for him mixed with outrage and sadness that my therapist had now vanished forever. Josh was making me the therapist, telling me of his long-held pain that reached right back to the time when I had been a client who knew nothing of this. Furthermore, the circumstances he described were shocking to me: Josh, a person who had helped so many others come back to life, telling me he had lived for many years contrary to his own wisdom. My hero was as utterly human and vulnerable as myself.

It was inevitable that Will would discover Josh's texts. I made no attempt to hide my phone and Josh texted so often. Far too often. Will was hurt and angry when he saw Josh's wordy, emotional texts asking to see me and expressing how he felt. Will retreated, walled himself in and asked me a thousand angry questions over and over. I was mortified and guilty. Although I had not succumbed to Josh's seduction, I knew a part of me wanted to. I hated myself for this in a way I hadn't hated myself in years.

I told Will about my conversations with Josh, what Josh had said about his life and what he had said about his feelings for me. I told him about the day in the rain. Will asked me how I felt about Josh and I admitted to getting closer to him emotionally than was safe. I said that I hadn't wanted to tell Will because I knew that I would have to cut contact altogether and I didn't want to. I couldn't let go because of who he had been to me for so long.

I asked Josh to stop calling and for a short time he did, but the damage was already done to my vulnerable marriage. Then, after only a week, Josh resumed his texting campaign, asking me not to be angry or shut him out any longer, telling me he *needed* me.

Will intercepted the texts and asked me if I had sexual feelings for Josh. I couldn't lie. I did. It was written all over me. I was so deeply ashamed, so sorry, yet unable to keep it a secret any longer.

Will seethed with resentment and hurt, knowing I had been unable to find those feelings for him. He told me our marriage was over and I had to get out of the house. I was afraid, I was tired and, to tell the truth, I was relieved it was all out. I went to my mum's house with our three-year-old. Will would barely speak to me. He would not listen either, not even on the phone. He simply hung up before I could say anything more than 'hello'.

Over the next weeks it was as if the ground beneath Will's faultlines opened beneath him. Despite me being only a relatively recent event in his life, I would, from that time on, feel blamed for every imperfection his life had ever witnessed. In the coming weeks he reunited with people he had previously blamed for his pain and banished from his life for almost a decade. I took their place as the source of hurt.

I look back now and it is crystal clear to me that Will and I could never have worked in the long term. We were awful together. I felt sad and flat with him and I'm sure he felt unattractive around me and deeply sad and resentful. We had been caught in a long, miserable spiral of avoidance and resentment around sex for years and we just didn't manage to face it.

Author Harville Hendrix describes marriage as 'the practice of becoming passionate friends' – combining both intense best-friendship and sexual aliveness. We didn't have what it took as a team and although I'd long suspected this, I'd been mute out of shame, fear and uncertainty about what was even possible for me. I take a great deal of responsibility for what happened.

Your faultlines never really disappear although they may be worn down, obscured or filled in. Grass grows over them; wind, water, wisdom and time reshape them; but they're there, they're there. Know where they are. Tread gently. Stay mindful but never choose safety alone over pleasure, over joy, over laughter. Your wounds can also be the sources of your wisdom and inspiration for your growth. Don't fear them. Respect them.

As you negotiate your path through your faultlines, balance caution with the thrill of adventure in your imperfect landscape. There's a fine line between the thrill of passionate engagement and fear of dying from its loss. You can't make all your choices out of fear, especially choices in love, and expect a perfect ending.

The end of our marriage was devastating, the end of an era, but it was an era that needed to end. I was sad not so much about the demise of the relationship, but about the *way* in which it ended. It was the antithesis of any ending I could ever have imagined for us. I cared for Will and I believe he cared for me but our life together smashed and burned so suddenly and hideously that there was little room for sentiment, only physical and emotional survival.

~

My patient Oliver allowed me to see how my life might have turned out had Will and I stayed together. Oliver's and my path intersected a number of times in odd ways. He and I attended the same drama school but didn't meet, then he became a patient for about four years. Later we lived in the same suburb with our kids mixing in the same circles.

Oliver came to me for therapy for depression and distress over his marriage to Kate. It sounded as though they had ingrained unhealthy emotional habits and no sex to boot, but he felt bonded to her by a long parallel life together. I felt great empathy for Oliver because the relationship he described was so similar to my marriage to Will. They'd wanted kids and it had been a FOMO marriage like mine, chosen using the 'better the devil you know' and 'we're nearly out of time' algorithms.

When I started to make different life choices from Oliver while he was still my patient I had to be extremely mindful as a therapist not to inadvertently influence him in a way that reflected my preferences rather than his. It turned out I didn't have to worry about unduly influencing him because, although we frequently discussed the serious difficulties he and Kate faced and his desire to end their marriage, he never acted upon it. His reward for staying was the second child they so dearly wanted and the stability and financial benefits of maintaining life with the same partner. I gained other things but not that precious second child that I too had wanted so much.

Different costs, different rewards, neither right nor wrong. Never sweat a definitively 'right' answer, just pursue your best answer.

It's strange how it goes in the end. People often play out crises according to their own scripts and assumptions, panicking and flying off the handle rather than listening and responding to what is actually happening. The times when life as we know it comes smashing down are the most vital times to stay mindful so we can emerge emotionally intact, albeit changed by the loss. However, they are the times most often disassociated from sense or compassion and characterised by rage, panic and flailing reactivity.

I did my yoga and kept myself together as best as I could, trying to avoid any unnecessary changes to the pre-schooler routine. I was devastated about losing our home and family, but ambivalent and confused about whether we should try to reconstitute the marriage. I asked Will to attend counselling so we could talk about our child, but talks quickly broke down. I asked Will to let me come back to the house while we assessed our future, but he would have none of it. I was terrified of the effects on our child, the loss of his home and intact family, but I was somewhat relieved to finally stop chasing the mirage that our marriage could be something other than it was.

At the local cafe, in the park, from a neighbour I met in the supermarket queue I heard whispers that I had left my marriage for my psychiatrist. Gradually, talk about my long-term affair reached me. I felt like I'd been placed in stocks in the town square: witch, harlot, madwoman. In actual fact, I was living in a tiny room at my mum's sleeping next to my pre-schooler, wondering what the hell had happened and where to go next.

I tried to put my attention everywhere but on Josh, yet every night I lay awake thinking about him and wondering if my ex-therapist could really be my partner instead of a fantasy. I became more intensely focused and efficient in everything else, to keep away from the desire that was burning and writhing inside me. My daily life as a full-time pre-school mum was all about my child, but for a few hours of consulting when Mum cared for him. Motherhood grounded me in love and simplicity because, above all else, I needed to keep life beautiful for my son.

The end of a marriage is the end of so much more than just the relationship between two people. It can re-arrange entire family structures, change the landscape of children's lives, cut faultlines, break hearts. Breaking up is not easy but damage can be minimised through mindfulness, compassion and keeping mutual kindness a top priority. Few couples manage those things seamlessly, but they're good goals to help people cope with difficult changes, especially children.

When adults behave kindly and respectfully to one another through separation and divorce, decades of research confirms that the kids enjoy the same outcomes on average as kids from intact families. It's family violence, conflict, abuse and chaos that hurts kids, whether their parents are together or not.

15

MISGUIDED LOVE

We learn geology the morning after the earthquake.

RALPH WALDO EMERSON

Josh went overseas for almost three weeks but as soon as he returned he began a campaign of fiercely pursuing me romantically. Love words fell from his lips and tears of horror and pleasure fell from my eyes. Wandering around alone on Broken Heart Beach much of the time, I desperately longed to feel his comfort, although he'd contributed to the pain. I felt powerless for so many reasons, real and imagined.

Such is the power of the relationship between a therapist and an ex-patient. He simultaneously elevated me to shining goddess with his attention, and diminished me to a shaking child on the inside by morphing unapologetically from father-figure to pursuer.

Finally, his persistence got the better of me and we met for lunch on a work day. We hugged as we met in the street and he kissed me.

He said he felt in love and stricken, thinking about me endlessly. It was bliss to my ears and blinding terror to the rest of me. He said that he felt weak and vulnerable, sometimes frightened by his feelings, but he knew he had to be with me. He said he felt deeply alive again because he loved me. He told me he had never felt this way before, never felt so intensely for a woman. I wanted to freeze that moment so it could never go further. I had heard all I had ever wanted to hear, and way too much more.

It dawned on me that despite the sick fear in the pit of my stomach, a part of me was soaring, satisfied, victorious. I had apparently won his love in no small way *despite* a decade of showing him every scar, every permutation of self-loathing I could come up with. I had unearthed the holy grail, but this wasn't how I thought it would be.

You can't have a normal sexual relationship with your therapist, even years later, even if you think you can – even though you so want to. Having that kind of relationship with someone who has been at the unequal level of trusted father-figure for you is going to feel abusive and incestuous to some part of yourself, *even if* it feels great in other parts. The price is too high.

I loved Josh with all my heart but the complexity of our relationship would always influence our landscape.

It was misguided to think otherwise. I dropped my map for a while and was lost again stumbling about in the Mirages where everything is more complex and twisted than you'd hoped, where aspects that look wonderful and hopeful can morph into darker realities as you approach. I loved Josh for everything he had given me but I was angry at how much he had taken in return. I felt intensely conflicted: victorious *and* ripped off, empowered *and* conquered, enthralled *and* appalled. I was in love and enraged at him, proud of being loved by him, yet so let down and wishing none of it had happened.

Then there was the sudden, emotionally violent way my marriage had broken. Mount Danger had erupted and obliterated the imperfect but stable little land we had inhabited as a family. I felt enormous guilt for the pain I had caused Will and for distress that might come to my son from the schism. I visited Blame City many times after leaving it years ago and swearing I'd never return. I considered taking up residence there, but it wasn't a healthy place to bring up my son. However, finding forgiveness of myself, for my feelings, for my decisions, for my weaknesses, for my faultlines and the mess they had led me into was difficult.

It didn't help that I was also confronted with the bitter judgements of others. A couple of mums who I'd thought were my friends stopped calling for playdates and coffees. A previously friendly local dad blatantly shunned me in the playground where we used to chat while our children played. I could only guess they had heard rumours and decided that I was guilty of ... of what, I'm not sure.

I was judged and apparently found guilty, at least of threatening their worlds. They simply cut me off without discussing it with me. Oddly, both the women were religious – churchgoing Christians. I had been under the impression that their religion is all about forgiveness, helping people when they're down and leaving judgement to a higher power. I guess they just weren't great ambassadors when it came to walking the talk of their spirituality.

Forgiveness, particularly of yourself, is such a complex process. I likened it to walking in a huge forest where there are clear, sunny patches followed by dark, dank, miserable hollows. In the Forest of Forgiveness you may have to pass through many hollows of shadiness then sun before you're finally in the clear.

~

Some years ago, a woman called Carla came to see me. Carla's marriage to an abusive husband had ended after he gambled away their home with loans and credit cards. She had three children, the oldest a profoundly autistic thirteen-year-old girl who had never spoken a word and couldn't care for herself. Carla felt intense anger towards her ex-husband, towards the girl, life and herself.

'If I don't find a way to forgive, to accept my life with all its shit, I'm going to go insane,' she told me.

Clearly, the forgiveness Carla needed was not the kind where someone says, 'I'm sorry.' It was a whole different animal; something far more profound, something much deeper.

As I worked with Carla on finding some peace, I saw just how long and irregular the path to forgiveness can be. Forgiveness isn't really about blame or saying sorry but about the process of deciding to come out of pain, so the unfair past can be left in the forest and we can fully and positively live in the *clear*. The forgiveness path winds in and out of acceptance and compassion back and forth through shadowy blame and anger. One day we feel our anger is gone, but the next day something triggers it and it's two steps forward, one step back. That's how human beings work. Life is not a straight line.

When you need to forgive to get free of the past there's often a part of you that doesn't want to let yourself or another person off the hook too easily. Resistance happens whenever we enter a process of change and growth. The desire to punish can keep you stuck, feeling like a victim, unwittingly locked in an invisible prison. But you can soothe yourself by understanding that forgiveness isn't condoning hurtful behaviour. It doesn't mean letting someone off the hook for what they did because they still have to deal with their own guilty head. It doesn't mean letting *yourself* off the hook easily either. Moving on authentically takes hard work.

Walking beside Carla, I learned that forgiveness can't take away all pain, it can't heal all ills or rectify life's injustices; but it can get us closer to liking ourselves, accepting reality and finding greater emotional freedom. Forgiveness can help us find a way to live, even when our pain is driving our daily emotional bus, by channelling the pain into ideas that support our values and create a better future.

As for forgive and forget – forget it. You can't make yourself forget and it's healthier not to try. Better to be mindful of your feelings rather than repress them, because if we try to push feelings away and pretend they're not there, they have a way of returning. Real forgiveness results in freedom; in a more peaceful state of mind; in reaffirming your values and resetting your boundaries, even after they've been violated. Even if you violated them yourself.

I worked with Carla and her daughter's caseworker, teachers and therapists to compile a submission for disability support for the girl's future. Meanwhile Carla began to find the courage and resources to face dealing with the dire situation her ex-husband had left her in emotionally and financially. She moved to a smaller home with the children but found good friends and more support nearby than she had experienced before.

She began to reach out to people and to get involved with the children's schools.

Gradually Carla felt other emotions aside from rage at her ex-husband, her daughter and herself; gradually she emerged from victimhood and Blame City. Mindfulness practice helped her to largely let go of the tranquillisers she had been relying on to suppress her panic and rage. She just kept one pill always in her purse, in case of emergency. She knew it would gradually lose its potency and then she would throw it away.

Forgiveness is for the strong who are ready to be the heroes of their own lives. It's not for those who want to stay victims. Choosing forgiveness means connecting to your soul, even in tough or conflicted times, repeatedly shaking off the chains of self-criticism and self-pity and walking with your pain towards the future, until your pain sends you on ahead without it.

16

LOVE AND LOSS

I am convinced that life is ten percent what happens to me, and ninety percent how I react to it.

CHARLES SWINDOLL

As Bob Marley once said, you don't know how strong you are until being strong is your only choice. Paul and Alison knew too much about love and loss. I was inspired by their love story and shaken by their misfortune.

They got engaged when they were both twenty-six. Paul lived with two mates in an old walk-up apartment in the inner city. He worked at a nearby bar and always had a lot of friends around to go out with after work. He was tall, slim, handsome, crazy in love with Alison and life was good. He was considering going back to university to study law, but not just yet. There was too much fun to be had.

Graphic artist Alison had a beautiful face and long, straight, dark hair. She favoured vintage dresses and wore a flower in her hair. She didn't mind a drink but not as much as Paul so when he went out with a bunch of people one wet, wintery Friday night Alison didn't go.

She was woken that night by a call from Paul's flatmate, James, who had called an ambulance for her fiancé and was with him in the hospital. James had found Paul bleeding and unconscious on the footpath at the bottom of the steep concrete stairs leading to their door. Apparently Paul had tripped and likely somersaulted down the wet stairs in the dark. It wasn't a huge fall, only about a metre and a half, but it was a very bad fall. His back was broken. It emerged over the following days and weeks that Paul was going to remain paralysed from almost the neck down.

Alison told me she was so grateful that James had found Paul that night as otherwise he may have died in the street alone. She was also grateful that she and Paul were already engaged when the accident happened so that for her there could be no question of them staying together. As far as she was concerned, they had decided to be together forever, they were still in love and even this loss couldn't stop them.

She told me their story over dinner at a restaurant with mutual friends, speaking in a soft but matter-of-fact tone. They'd been married fifteen years when I met them. Paul ran a small online business from home and Alison had successfully developed her design business. I was taken with her openness and clarity. It was apparent that Alison drew on their love story as a source of strength and resilience in the face of their losses and pain.

There were so many other ways she might have constructed, told and retold the narrative of their Lovelands journey – through lenses of unfairness, victimhood or bad timing. But Alison seemed to understand the power of story to shape reality. She had chosen to see their journey as heroic, unstoppable under pressure and built on love. I heard Paul remark that night, laughing at something Alison said, that he still had a lot to live for. They'd lost so much but they'd held on to one another, held on to love.

～

I couldn't hold on to Josh. Three months into our relationship Josh was diagnosed with prostate cancer on a routine visit to the GP. Over the weeks it became apparent that his cancer was rare, aggressive and had advanced throughout his body.

I made him organic food. I researched every complementary therapy known to humankind and then some. I juiced, he juiced, we did it all. We detoxed him, employed homeopathic remedies and took recommended supplements. I helped him to meditate and practise some basic yoga, but it was already very late on his journey.

I had wanted him to be the immortal beloved, the hero, the saviour who wiped out the pain of the past; but he was just a man and suffering and death was coming to him as it does to everyone, without favour. Unwittingly, I was catapulted into being my own hero. Not a superhero with amazing powers, just my own everyday source of very fallible human strength, because there was no other resource. Not only would I have no guide from here on, but *I* would be the guide for *my* former guide. I would lead both of us through the Plains of Uncertainty, through experiences stranger and more frightening than either of us had ever seen in all our travels.

We had an intensely terrible and intensely beautiful two years together because we had so much in common and knew each other so well. We had a lust to eat up everything we could because we knew we were on the clock. We talked about everything unreservedly and very rarely hit conflict because we both wanted to give, not take. He called it rare beauty. We were secure and deep in our commitment to the end of his days and we knew this time was coming soon. From diagnosis throughout treatment, we received no positives from the medical team, not one. The cancer was simply too advanced.

We took nothing for granted, everything was a celebration created to keep darkness in its miserable place for another day, another night. He said many times how, ironically, he'd been living a 'dead' life for years, but now that everything else in his life had changed for the better, he was under the threat of actual death. I learned from being with him, as he blossomed mentally and spiritually while physically withering, that, for some of us, the threat of imminent death is less frightening than living a flat, passionless life.

Somehow, by the force of our souls we made days romantic, funny and happy despite, or because of, death's steady march towards us. Josh re-embraced literature, having not read much for years, and we talked about people's stories over leisurely dinners.

Various treatments failed and the fear increased steadily. Still, we stubbornly hung on to every opportunity for fun. Josh bought front-row tickets for Liza Minnelli but found himself in hospital a few days before. He got special permission to leave hospital and attend Liza's performance with me, on the condition that I brought him straight back to the hospital afterwards. Unfortunately he was on 'nil by mouth' at the time, but it didn't stop him from buying me a glass of wine and rubbing some on his lips like lip balm. It made him really happy and it made me laugh.

Liza blew my mind and I found myself sobbing with overwhelming emotion because here was a person of fantasy and legend, right here, reaching out her arms and flipping her lashes. When she sang 'Maybe This Time' Liza looked me straight in the eye for just a moment and so much of my past seemed to fuse with the present. I was transported back to a young girl who'd wanted to be an actress, who longed to be loved and adored, gazing transfixed at a video of *Cabaret* in a '70s lounge room. Liza's anthemic, optimistic song about surely having to win at love *sometime* after losing so many times was always one of my favourites. What a sting there was in the tail to hear it that night, well along the path to another loss.

The week I admitted Josh to palliative care was the week my little boy started school. I clung to the happy, the innocent, the tiny bits I could enjoy and control in life, while partnering Josh through the relentless chaos of disease and dying. With the support of my mother I kept my child completely separated from this hell, a mighty juggling act in itself, and my kid's sweetness gave me lightness and the only hope that some semblance of normality still existed beyond Josh's pain. I split my dwindling energy between single motherhood, seeing my patients, nursing my dying lover and keeping myself afloat. I realised that I was stronger than I had ever imagined I could be.

On a Sunday morning I felt him with me, full of love, holding and kissing and comforting me in my dream. I thought it was really happening in my half-sleep, but he had been largely unconscious for days. I woke to hear him moaning in his bed. I called the nurses. Josh died quietly with his hand in mine.

One of the most difficult things about helping someone on their journey towards death is that you may not agree with the paths they want to take, the things they want said and done and the things they don't. For example, Josh did not accept that the end of his life was approaching in the realistic, empowered way of my former patient Lily.

Josh didn't want to know, he didn't want to hear, he didn't want to talk about dying. I respected his wishes, of course, but his choices did not make our journey any easier. In fact, it meant that I often felt at a loss to help him in deep ways because he wouldn't let us map this strange new place, wouldn't let me carry a compass or plan ahead for how to cope with new challenges. All he wanted was for me to stay beside him for as long as possible while he tried to row frantically against the current of the River of Life as it carried him downstream.

We don't always have power to decide our circumstances and the challenges that befall us on our journey, but we *do* have the power to choose whether we face them head on or run and hide. We author that part of our story, we decide who to be in the face of success and defeat.

I understood that Josh's fear got the better of him and he needed to write the end of his story his way. Although I didn't agree with his denial as a method of coping and it flew in the face of what he'd taught me in therapy about empowering yourself, I understood that he was doing the best he could. I respected his right to do it his way. There are as many ways to die as there are to live.

I could still feel him with me long after he stopped breathing, after his boat had left the river and disappeared over the horizon back to the Sea of Bliss Dreams. I could feel we had some different kind of togetherness. Death does not end our relationship with a loved one when it takes them from us. The relationship continues to exist in us, perhaps forever. Death happens far too easily to really be the end of the story.

17

LOVE AND GRIEF

Though lovers be lost, love shall not; And death shall have no dominion.

DYLAN THOMAS

The bereavement counsellor at the hospital offered me a story of dragonflies as a metaphor for the different realms of life and afterlife. She said:

> Swimming in the water the dragonfly larvae are curious about the air and space above the water because they cannot see it clearly. The only way to get to it is to die as a 'swimmer' and become a 'flyer'.
>
> Once you're a 'flyer' you can't go back into the water or you die. And so, there are different realms for different levels of existence and you can only experience each in turn, in nature's time.

It was beautiful. I believed in her metaphor but it was no help at all. I got so tired of my head, being in grief, riding the rollercoaster of loss again and again. I refocused my attention over and over, read a book with my son, did some colouring, worked out that night's dinner ... *I can do this*, I would tell myself, *I can do this*.

For four months after Josh died I did little but mother my son, take him to school, care for him, and grieve. I lived in an otherwise grey world: I wrote, I grief-journalled, I asked the universe for guidance and help because I didn't know what else to do.

Just keep holding on to myself and my kid, I would tell myself, keep holding on one moment longer until this moment is memory and hope that the next moment will be better. I knew that feelings ebb and flow, I knew that no matter how bad I felt it couldn't stay exactly the same forever, but it was so hard to find relief.

Something I noticed in deepest grief (and this was absolutely not all the time) was a sense of being more fully and intensely present in the flow of things, moment by moment. Grief kicked along my mindfulness of the ever-shifting, quickly morphing nature of my thoughts and feelings, and the power of my senses to affect my inner state.

Grief sharpened my sensitivity to everything I heard, sensed and saw. Lightning-fast connections ran from sensory input to emotion-charged memories at the slightest hint of something that reminded me of the loss. In grief, time took on a Dali-esque quality, sometimes dragging, sometimes racing, and on occasion warping. A scent could send me back two years in a nanosecond, a piece of music or an object I glanced at could transport me into the full emotional experience of a specific moment in the past. When it finished, I'd be back in the super-reality of now, shaken and stirred, having to say, 'That was then, this is now', and take a breath.

In *A Grief Observed*, C.S. Lewis records his struggle after the death of his wife. He writes about how grief compels us to question our core beliefs about a Higher Power, God or an afterlife because there is no certainty about anything in this world; and, it seems, little justice or mercy for inevitable losses and suffering. In grief we confront the utterly incomprehensible, asking the gaping agony of silence, 'Where are you my love? Can you hear me? This can't be the end forever, can it?'

In darkest grief it felt like a black hole was pulling me in. I was gut-wrenchingly lonely and financially exposed because Josh left a lot of things undone. Vultures smelled the combined scents of death and financial disarray and circled. The days following a death direct the harsh lens of ultimate reality on those left behind so that you can see right through their skin; you see what they're made of, how they behave when they're hungry, sad and alone. I saw through many people as they disappeared; as stuff disappeared with them. The old life dissolved.

Winter was long.

Then, unexpectedly, I triumphed.

Not over people: those who loved continued to love; those who hated continued to hate. Nor did I triumph over death. We all die one day.

I triumphed by being catapulted body and soul into realising that our physical time is utterly limited and when it finishes you won't be ready unless you live every day how you want to be remembered. Death taught me that every moment is throbbing with possibility. There's no time to waste being anything but an embodiment of your values and core desires, immersed in what lights you up. It taught me that if you're not in pain, you're lucky; and if you are in pain, it's best to deal with it sooner rather than later.

Death taught me that life is so much simpler than we make it out to be. There's no time for resentment-building in relationships; no time for being cruel, small-minded or greedy. And to be that way is delusional because it will play out through the seeds you sow, the energy of your soul. There's no time to hurt intentionally, to create damage. There's not even any point. That kind of victory is a death and there's no time for death in life.

From death, I learned to live passionately, to live kindly, to love like there's no tomorrow because everything else is a waste of our precious time.

Josh gave me some treasures that I could only fully appreciate when he was gone. Most of all, he helped diminish my fear of death and left in its place an appreciation of life that I never knew before. A deep gratitude for being alive, being well and having purpose and love became my primary state of mind as the grief began to ease.

I was not always this woman. I was once a sad, angry girl. He left me knowing that I am tough, I am able to be the hero, the carer, the survivor. He helped save me and I helped save him. He left me with a sense that he is still present, that there must be a certain, somehow energetic life after death because I feel a presence with me that I cannot deny. Although I am not sure what it is or how to explain it, the presence gives me great comfort.

Those fault-marred badlands that drove me into therapy are peaceful. They're awesome and powerful, they beckon sometimes, but the agony and terror have gone and can never be there again in the way that they were. A peace has been revealed in me that when I am connected to it is so complete that I want for nothing.

Josh's suffering, his losses, his death, woke me up to life, woke me up to what is important. His death left me grateful, more courageous, more compassionate, grown-up and alone. For some months it left me to figure out the mad complexity of grief and how the hell to get through it.

What can we possibly do to help ourselves bear grief and keep moving through it?

We can reach out in relationships where we can regularly, consistently share our rollercoaster feelings that connect us to a common sense of being. Connecting with others reminds us that someone else, at some time, has felt a similar way and borne it. Although you have never felt more alone, countless other people are feeling grief too, right now.

Objects and symbols can be places to focus emotions so you don't have to hold everything internally, which can relieve some pain pressure inside.

Rituals, private or formalised, may hold a place in honouring and remembering all that is grieved for. Grief is never so simple as to be for a person alone. It is also for an entire unique shared world.

Writing in a journal or other creative expression can also help, a little. I was a prolific writer in grief, trying to make sense of what I was going through by getting it out of me and looking at it on paper, in the light of day. Later, when I had recovered enough to edit and share some parts of that writing, Arianna Huffington published it in *The Huffington Post*. Many people reached out to share their experience of grief with me because they knew from my writing that I would hear their grief in all its intensity.

Coping with grief is less about doing, knowing or understanding anything than it is about space to just be with what is, to sit with mystery. It is the part of life and evolution where we are forced to tolerate loss and uncertainty, to accept the incomprehensible nature of things and to let go of our desire to want to make sense of everything when sometimes, we just can't. It's a time when tuning into 'being' mind offers more chance of relief than 'doing' mind because you cannot think your way out of grief, no matter how clever you are.

None of us wants to be friends with grief, but we can't avoid meeting it and getting to know it at some stage. It's important to hold the perspective that we are never the only one experiencing it, but it is a normal part of the process to feel that way, a lot. Coping with grief is an exercise in surviving each moment, honouring the gravity of what we're going through, rolling with myriad feelings, being with what is, and getting plenty of support.

When you sail the River of Life with someone you love who's en route to the end, they let you off at Broken Heart Beach, then go on alone. You might've landed there a few times at endings, sunburnt and thirsty with thorns under your feet and the sun in your eyes. There are cliffs of grief and sadness, and faultlines run dangerously close to the water.

Sit there on a rock for a while if you want to, look at the sea, pick your way over the rocky shores. Solitude and reflection on Broken Heart Beach is a stage in the complex and diverse processes of grief, but you can't stay there alone too long. The weather is stormy and dark and there's little shelter along the jagged cliffs. You just have to get up, even when you don't feel strong enough.

There is a balance between allowing yourself quiet time to be and feel, and getting back into the world, engaging with others again. Before too many nights and days have passed you must trek back into the interior of the Lovelands. Look for a place that feels right, a new opportunity to stretch yourself back into life, a place to recover – a Resilience Retreat. There you can remember how to reconnect with your strengths.

When you face an ending, remember the River of Flow and the experiences that are always waiting there for you. Return always to your oases of strength and support. Immerse yourself in self-compassion, in giving, in flow. Love is the greatest healer, even for the loss of love.

18

LOVE AS LIFE FORCE

Bad things will happen and good things too. Your life will be full of surprises. Miracles happen only where there has been suffering. So taste your grief to the fullest. Don't try and press it down. Don't hide from it. Don't escape. It is life too. It is truth. But it will pass and time will put a strange honey in the bitterness. That's the way life goes.

BEN OKRI

If you surrender to the experience of loss but stay open to the possibility of healing, inland from Broken Heart Beach you will find your Resilience Retreat. It's a place to stop, find new streams of flow and access your unconquerable spirit.

One night I fell on my knees and leaned on my bed with my head in my hands and said to the universe: 'I surrender to a force greater than myself. Take everything I have, any gifts I can offer: my profession, my learning, my years of therapy and my rocky path to here. What I've been through must be good for something; take all I have to offer. I have no idea where to go or what to do from here. I am completely lost. Just take me, take it all. I will do what I am led to do with all I have. I trust it will help others, help my son and help me. Just let me be useful.'

A day or two later, a job alert email arrived in my inbox; it was a psychologist job in a church. The minister was a well-known psychotherapist who talked of faith in terms of human wellbeing and defined God as a non-interventionist Presence rather than a man in the clouds.

I'd never had anything to do with churches, but my world was on its head and I was up for new experiences. Going back to being a general psychologist, counselling people in crisis as I had done for years, no longer felt possible and I also needed a break from working with distressed couples. There was so much weight on my shoulders as a single mum without trying to carry the burdens of the world. I needed a broader psychological role, perhaps bringing in my wider background, and this highly unusual advertisement seemed to describe just that, and at just the right time.

I met the minister, Francis Macnab, at the first inter-view and we liked each other right away. He was funny and a naturally gracious person but his trickster bent was evident immediately. He noted that I had worked with 'that other mob up the road', meaning Relationships Australia, and he knew the previous GP who had operated

the medical clinic where I had conducted my private practice. His knowledge of Melbourne past and present was
extensive and his mind razor sharp. He'd been minister
of St Michael's for forty years at that time and head of
the Cairnmillar Institute, a private psychology college, for
about fifty years. Like most people, I was astonished to
discover he was over eighty and working full-time plus.

I got the job of his collaborator in thought-leadership
and program creation: to develop and manage wellbeing
programs, and write and speak about spirituality and
wellbeing. No one could have been more surprised than I
was at how quickly Dr Macnab and I fell into working so
comfortably together.

I could see that religion was no longer in its heyday
but the search for practical, personal spirituality and
the hunger for social connection and personal growth
opportunities were as strong as ever. So, I pulled together
my knowledge and resources as a yoga and mindfulness
teacher as well as a psychologist and, with a few dynamic
colleagues, we created a broad wellbeing program that
included courses, classes, events, lectures and groups,
forming a secular outreach to the people of Melbourne,
beyond the church community.

St Michael's is one of the oldest churches in Melbourne.
The air inside vibrates with history and, despite the
discord of the thousands of humans who have passed
through it, there is an inexplicable benevolent peace and

presence there. At risk of sounding woo-woo, I actually felt physically supported by the air around me when I occasionally took to the high pulpit as a guest speaker for Dr Macnab. It was extraordinary and the sense it gave me right to my bones was that, at *that* time and in *that* way, I was exactly where I was supposed to be, doing exactly what I was supposed to do.

Speaking regularly in front of hundreds of people made me more courageous but it was also an incredible experience of flow. I discovered I could kind of emotionally crowd-surf, which took the fear out of it. If I surrendered to it and let myself feel supported by the energy of the room and my preparation, it more or less fell into place.

There was one vital condition to flow for me, something that made it entirely different from an acting performance – the material had to feel utterly authentic to me, streamed live from my soul, and I had to own it one hundred per cent in the telling.

We were a success. The centre became a finalist in the City of Melbourne Awards for contribution to community in its first year of operation. I thought of Josh every day but I focused on motherhood and building the centre as my priorities. In some ways I was tougher, more resilient from what I'd been through; in other ways, I was very raw.

The church community presented plenty of opportunities for building my resilience that I'd not encountered before. I had to look death in the eye regularly; most church congregations in Australia are getting older and members are dying. I took part in, and cried through, numerous funeral rituals. They never got easier but I came to accept them as a part of life and how it ends.

As Dr Macnab's retirement approached it was time for me to return to my own practice, but we remained firm friends. In my four years there I observed and felt so deeply that, in the end, love is all that matters. It's love alone that is the life force, the energy behind resilience and healing across the timeline of our journey as we gather the wisdom of our Lovelands – past, present and future.

The wisdom of the past is that there is so much power in knowing where you come from emotionally, what shaped you and the kinds of experiences that remind you of pain or feel as though they open up the faultlines of your inner landscape. Knowing where the faultlines lie means you can be self-compassionate and ready to look after yourself when life takes you too near them.

Finding peace around the past means, first of all, accepting that what happened did happen, however wrong or sad or unfair some experiences were. They happened and we can't change that. Awareness and insight into the past allow you to be prepared for what lies ahead around your faultlines. For example, you feel catapulted back to ancient places by some experiences, like catching a passing whiff of a familiar but horrible perfume. There's no time to think – you're just back there, suddenly feeling small and hopeless. The original pain can be too old to be in focus, covered by layers of sediment, now dissolved into a solution and made potent from years of fermentation.

Being mindful around your past, and how past pain can be triggered, allows you to have strategies for coping, soothing yourself and getting support. It's empowering to be able to say, 'Hello, old friend' to old feelings and faultlines without fearing they'll overwhelm you.

Finding a place for the events of your life, locating them in your story, empowers you. You choose where to place them. You choose to look at them, when and from which perspective, and you choose to move on to the next thing in your landscape when you're ready. You choose how much attention you want to give to various experiences in defining who you are and how you operate, once you become aware of their existence and impacts.

When you're able to remember that traumas or pain of the past are in the past, you can deal more clearly with your thoughts and feelings in the here and now and stay present rather than getting lost in the inner badlands. Resilience is bolstered by focusing on two kinds of actions in the present moment: what you're great at, and what you love.

When you focus on your strengths, you remind yourself that you're an accomplished person with skills and achievements and that you're empowered in your life. When you focus on doing things you love, you can open the door to flow. Being engaged and present in the moment pulls you out of memories and fantasies and immerses you in the moment of now.

Grab the opportunity for fresh adventures and new experiences that excite you; they will keep reminding you who you are and keep you passionate and expanding. Those adventures might be in the wilds or they may be in a chair – there is no place more vast and limitless than your mind when you focus on living now and harnessing your strengths and passions.

It's essential to remain open to a better future even in the darkest of moments. The hardest thing about trauma, depression, anxiety – indeed, any unhelpful state of mind – is the feeling, or worse still, the belief, that the hard time will never end. Depression or intense anxiety can temporarily narrow your field of vision, preventing you from seeing better possibilities or the hope of a brighter future. When things are dark you tend to forget that feelings ebb and flow by their very nature, that change will come. If we can remain present and mindful in adversity we can build courage and resilience, holding fast long enough to realise that all things pass.

Love, passionate engagement, aliveness, connection – these are the qualities we live to feel, these are the experiences that give meaning to life, relationships and work. Love is ultimately the life force that animates our being. Love saves us from getting lost, love gives us meaning in the wilderness. Self-love takes us home to ourselves, love for others unites us with our soul companions, passionately loved pursuits create meaning and purpose. Love is the essential energy and quality of presence in the ordinary moments of life that adds up to the sum of our days.

Some people just flow with love, few obstacles blocking their internal paths. Maybe they don't have many faultlines to struggle with, or more likely they're amazing rock-climbers who take the cliffs and chasms of the Lovelands joyfully in their stride.

One morning, when I was drinking coffee out of a takeaway cup and hanging out in the main church office three floors up, a window-cleaning guy dangling on a harness outside the window started waving to me through the glass. He had a big smile and surf-blond curls cascading from his helmet. He wasn't young but he was full of verve like a boy, apparently delighted to see me. The office girls turned to me with wide questioning eyes. It took me a moment, but I remembered him.

When I was acting, I did some radio work and hosted 'Soul to Soul', a New Age community radio show that explored spirituality. I was invited to take part in an energetic healing workshop in exchange for mentioning it on the radio. The workshop wasn't my thing but I met a boy called Warren who *was* my thing. I was with Pete back then so Warren and I became friends, nothing more, but he was a ray of light.

Warren was all dreamy sweetness, gentleness and wonder about the world. He rode a skateboard to get around and he worked as a window-cleaner in the city, abseiling skyscrapers. He was a highly skilled rock-climber and hanging in midair all day was completely natural to him. It was where he was happiest. One early morning he called me from thirty storeys up in a wild ecstasy about seeing some birds of prey. Apparently the wild creatures had nested in a nook on one of the city's tallest buildings. Being up high with those birds in the cold air, above it all, meant the world to him. Above the complex city, in the midst of it, Warren kept it simple and he was strikingly happy.

We'd lost touch long ago when he went to Nepal but here he was again, still abseiling buildings and loving it. Still the embodiment of life force. Some people are open channels. Some people just know how to *be* the love that they are.

It's a steep path to the Resilience Retreat, but once you get there you'll find the trek was worth it. You might make new friends or renew old acquaintances. There's time and space to remember your sense of purpose and reconnect with the energy of life. Love is that energy and energy never dies, it just changes form.

Hike often in the Forest of Forgiveness and feel its healing. Beyond the forest are new beaches with pristine sand, crystal-clear waters and temperate weather. You can bathe and warm yourself at Three Loves Beach – we'll head there now. The beach is named for the three great loves that pave the way to the best happiness we can find on earth: self-compassion, mindful relationships and experiencing flow.

19

—

THE THREE
GREAT LOVES

*Success is liking yourself, liking what you do, and liking
how you do it.*

MAYA ANGELOU

Becoming a therapist was an exhilarating, rewarding and, at times, challenging process of growing and finding my ways to be most helpful to people. I've worked with many brave and extraordinary patients at turbulent and critical times in their lives. I've been privileged to traverse their Lovelands with them and to see the huge variations and striking similarities in the inner landscapes and emotional experiences of humans.

My work has confirmed for me repeatedly the centrality of love in our lives. It has confirmed for me the vital influence of how we are loved as children, our attachment styles, in determining the quality of relationships we form later. It has shown me how self-compassion, mindful relationships and experiences of flow are keys to wellbeing.

Many times I've helped people to understand the value of greater self-awareness, becoming more mindful of the blocks and defences they allow to get in the way of love, and learning how to remove those impediments. I've walked with people in their badlands, feeling their terror and seeing firsthand how much they are struggling with their demons and how bravely they keep facing them. I've supported them to name those demons and to see that, once brought out of their caves and examined in the hard light of day, the demons aren't as ugly or as dangerous as they feared.

I've witnessed people grow in wisdom and step into new levels of emotional freedom, having made connections between their present pain and past traumas that had locked them wandering aimlessly in their badlands for years. I've seen people sigh with relief or cry with joy when they discover that they are not crazy, they are not shameful; that they are worthy, and that they have sovereignty over their bodies and their lives.

It became my area of expertise to help couples reconnect to their love stories, to unravel patterns of behaviour that didn't serve them and to understand how their histories may be impacting on their current relationship in unhelpful ways. A great gift of my own journey, especially time spent lost in my badlands, was the invaluable insight and empathy I gained from my own struggles. Real wisdom that's in your cells cannot be gained solely in a classroom or through living a mistake-free life, if such a life exists. Experience has taught me that forgiveness and taking responsibility are always helpful; regrets are not. My greatest mistakes, failings and scars are among the most important and majestic landmarks of my Lovelands – they have ultimately signposted the way to a passionate and beautiful life.

Each couple must travel the Lovelands, risking the faultlines and mirages, mapping one another's landscape as well as their own. The trip can be fraught, especially if they wander very far apart and lose the connection they once had. It can be even harder if they wander so far into their badlands that empathy is lost and poisonous slag heaps of criticism, resentment and defensiveness mar their landscapes.

What has become very clear to me is that love isn't a mystery, it isn't airy-fairy or random as popular culture might have us think. Love, indeed all emotion, has its own logic; it just isn't the same kind of linear logic as our intellect employs. Love also has methods – ways to be, ways to live that embody purpose, pleasure and soul-felt joy – that give you a guide for traversing your Lovelands.

The best place to start is to understand that there are three fundamental loves of our lives: self-compassion; mindful relationships with others (be they a partner, beloved friends, family or other beings of any kind); and experiences of flow – pursuing the work or activities that compel you to immerse yourself in the bliss of doing and being. I have mentioned these three before, but here I've given them their own chapter to emphasise that they are the sum of love, the sum of us.

When these three are discovered and nurtured – when they become your focus – life feels whole. These three add up to a full, rich life of wellbeing, passion, emotional freedom and peak experiences. Our life's journey is ultimately an epic treasure-hunt for these three loves of our lives; and a process of developing the skills, wisdom and awareness to recognise your trinity of love, prioritise it and revel in it.

Self-compassion

Self-love or self-compassion seems to be the hardest love to find. It's much easier to focus on someone else, particularly romantically, and get excited about them as the pathway to your happiness. However, at some point you realise that nobody else can make you feel good about yourself or encourage you if *you* don't choose to internalise it and cut yourself some slack.

Self-compassion means affording yourself the same basic kindness that you would easily extend to others. By offering yourself some compassion when you make a mistake, you can recover faster from suffering, learn from the experience, more quickly regroup and gather the energy to forge ahead.

Holding a grudge, especially against yourself, shuts down your energy and means you have to fight much harder to recover from a negative experience than if you were to give yourself some understanding and encouragement.

Self-compassion means recognising we're all in life, love and suffering *together* – all beings are united in living, failing and triumphing. You're not to be singled out and judged more harshly – not even by you. We are each unique and yet, in some ways, in the *significant* ways, we are all equal and worthy of compassion.

When we're children, we depend on adults to lift us up, to soothe us, to help us get through emotional distress when things don't go our way. But as adults it's necessary to take the lead in caring for ourselves emotionally.

The first step in creating better relationships, whether they be couple relationships or any other kind, is to really know the shape of ourselves emotionally. Love flows in us naturally as the energy of life, but it can get diverted or blocked by our faultlines – our raw spots, fears and defences against threats.

Knowing, 'owning' and being compassionate with ourselves about the attachment wounds we carry diminishes some of the confusion and distress about why we behave as we do sometimes. It allows us to move on when we make mistakes and not waste time dwelling on our shortcomings or vulnerabilities.

When we're kind to ourselves our vulnerabilities can become our strengths. We can bathe in the Lake of Self-Compassion to soothe our rawness, then keep moving away from the seedy lure of Blame City.

In sum, self-compassion or self-love springs from self-awareness because knowing ourselves better means knowing how to take responsibility for our feelings and actions, how to stay with our values and look after ourselves emotionally as we would a child.

Passionate flow

Struggling to find passion in work or other pursuits is a common challenge. I always reassure patients that it is part of life to *discover* your passions and vocation; it is not something that many people just *know*. Even those who are sure early in life often change their career path a couple of times as they grow and mature as human beings.

The passions of your childhood may indeed stay with you all your life, but they may also expand with you or fall away and become redundant as you learn more deeply about yourself, your values and the way the world works. Visiting the River of Flow consistently throughout life keeps your life force and passions fresh, flexible and alive in you, opening up possibilities for further adventures and joys.

Mindful relationships

Third, there are relationships, not just with other people, but with any other beings who share something in life with you – be they animal or spiritual. Relationships can be challenging because we don't control all aspects; they involve others, which means they involve risk and navigating differences.

As I said, the first step in creating mindful relationships is to know ourselves; but we must also be able to hear the pain of others, the yearnings behind their words and behaviour. Mindful awareness and being able to soothe our own reactions will allow us to listen more fully to others, with a less defended heart, and therefore connect more deeply.

In disagreements, instead of going into terrible hurt over something, we might suddenly understand that what is difficult for *them* is really not about us.

You can let go of being reactive in life and instead focus on charting your own course and allowing others to do so too. You can let go of criticism of yourself and others.

Regularly spend time at Mindfulness Mountain to hone your experience of just *being.* Through that understanding in your every cell, you'll realise that you can decide to just *be* the love that you *are.*

20

FALLING IN LOVE

She wonders if this is what people call falling in love, the desire to be with someone for every minute of the rest of her life.

YIYUN LI

It starts with the excited realisation that this *hot* person is paying you a special kind of attention, looking at you in a certain way that's more intensely interested than you expected. A feeling of engaged anticipation comes over you so you feel pulled towards them, wanting to know more about them, wondering if it's going to be the lovely thing you think it is. Burning curiosity pairs with rushes of hormones that distract you from daily life and steal your appetite for food. The erotic imagination runs wild, scoping out potentialities, playing with fire, long before your wise mind might consider allowing any of it into reality.

～

A chapel attached to St Michael's has been recreated as a secular meditation sanctuary, a place of reflection open to all. Andrew had never been there before; he happened to wander in after visiting some stockbrokers in the office tower next door. I worked in the adjacent administration building and rarely visited the chapel, but that day I was there for just a few minutes. Those were the precise minutes Andrew walked in.

The chapel is a dim, otherworldly, stone-floored sacred space, the focus of which is a Japanese rock sculpture with water running over it into a small pool. A light, symbolising the promise of a new day, rises from the base of the eastern wall. It's a comforting cave characterised by the humble majesty and solidity of its central rock, a sandstone marked with deep faultlines, traced and soothed by a delicate trickle of water.

A white piece of stone, carved to resemble a wing, rises towards a bright dome in the centre of the chapel above. It symbolises hope, rebirth, victory over suffering and rising from grief and pain into a radiant new life.

At St Michael's, I'd shared the meaning of the sculpture with many people, sitting with them, supporting their hope. Now, unexpectedly, astonishingly, it was suddenly my turn to feel elevated.

I told Andrew about the place, as I always did if someone showed an interest in it, and we talked about the rocks. He was a geologist, an explorer, the CEO of a gold mining company. I told him I was a psychologist, currently working for the church. Then we sank into a long, far-ranging conversation about deep things, difficult stuff, funny things. He asked me to have coffee and talk further another day. Since there was a cafe in the church courtyard it wasn't a big deal.

He made me laugh. A lot. It sounds like a small thing but at that time, it was the most important thing anyone could give me. I realised that I'd almost forgotten how to just laugh about silly stuff with another adult.

He'd faced a few challenges too. His long marriage had ended a year or so before, he travelled a great deal for work and he was looking for a sense of stability in life, not through a place, but in himself. I helped him to reflect on things differently, to put context and meaning around changes in his life and family.

We talked for a long while and quickly felt close, from different worlds of work and experience, but with a similar bliss-seeking spirit. Andrew is earthy, tanned, broad-shouldered and essentially masculine, a larrikin with a PhD. He's so different from Josh and the polar opposite of Will, so he felt exotic to me.

Having spent much of my life in conversations with actors, therapists, yogis, patients and plenty of moody types (!) I found Andrew's optimism and simple, unanalysed joy at being alive to be a revelation. His everyday happiness gradually changed the way I saw everything. Andrew just being Andrew enchanted me. With my introspection, yogic spirituality and tendency to think about psychodynamics a *lot*, I was exotic to Andrew too. He described me as a 'beautiful alien', which made me laugh.

We had lives full of experiences to share and the desire to explore each other's worlds and make our own together. We could have been best buddies from the first day we met, but it was impossible to look at him without noticing that his shirt covered hard muscle in his arms, that his smile connected directly with his heart. It was only going to one place right from the start.

We met again a few days later and talked all evening, not eating much out of absorption in conversation and a good dose of trembly excitement. We were the last to leave the restaurant and time had just dissolved around us magically. He gave me a brief hug at the car and I imagined, for just a second, merging completely with him. I never wanted to let go.

He was travelling regularly for work so he went away for a week, but as soon as he returned he asked for a second dinner together. I was really excited and quite surprised by how well we were hitting it off because I hadn't socialised with a man since Josh died. A part of me had thought that perhaps my romantic life would end there permanently, although this sounds really dumb looking back.

We tried to take it slowly because we had kids and responsibilities and the last thing I wanted was complications with a man and I told him so. There were no complications. It was all extraordinarily simple.

We had fun, we talked, we hung out with each other's families and we laughed and laughed ourselves into ever deeper intimacy and powerful connection. We consciously started building our own history, a history we knew we'd be proud of until the last.

Life unfolds a kind of soul family. We're drawn to particular people, thrown together repeatedly if we miss each other the first or second time, until our paths intersect. Andrew and I discovered that we had worked in the same small suburban office building at the same time about six years prior to meeting. He would have walked right past my office door every day to get to his own office. Although we never met back then, we would have been only metres away from each other countless times. Undoubtedly, we must have passed each other in the foyer or the cafe, never suspecting for a moment that we were brushing shoulders with the love of our lives.

On our first dates Andrew was more honest than he needed to be, telling me everything about his perceived faults rather than trying to minimise them like most people do. *I* absolutely tried to minimise mine. He was completely open about having strong feelings for me from the start. He didn't for a moment seem to consider playing it cool, or playing his feelings down. I was in awe of him for not having any need to be emotionally reserved, not caring about appearing self-possessed and powerful at the start of a relationship like most men I'd known. He was *all* in. Paradoxically it gave him more power; vulnerability equals strength. He wore his heart on his sleeve and I bowed to it internally and pledged to honour his openness and candour by matching it.

It wasn't difficult. Almost everything about being together was easy. After a couple of months we went to Seminyak and locked ourselves in a luxury retreat with a private pool, day beds, night beds, all kinds of beds, spas and exotic food.

I'd anticipated that the body infused by his soul would be aware, sensitive and sensual and it is. He's the quintessential tough guy with a beautiful, loving heart of devotion. I'm more at peace with a man than ever before.

So where are my faultlines? Oh, don't worry, they're there; but I am able to respond to them very differently. They maintain enough charge to occasionally cast a shadow in times of loneliness or stress but they haven't the power to weigh me down or choke me into a panic as they once did.

When you understand your raw spots enough to soothe them, you can find a new courage and freedom in that wisdom. Your self-awareness can help you to be kinder to yourself because you understand why you occasionally freak out a bit inside instead of wondering what's wrong with you. You can forgive your insecurities when you appreciate *why* you have them and understand them as a logical consequence of your attachment history. You can see that there's nothing wrong with you and that you are human, etched with your experiences, just as you should be.

A gift of the faultlines is that your erotic imagination, like a hot geothermal spring, typically bubbles close to them, flowing through openings they've created in the surface of you. It's understandable because the faultlines hold in them the yearning, longing, lusting for the love you most desire. Desire glows hot around experiences you feel you *need* urgently because you didn't have enough of them – non-negotiables like nurturing, acceptance, being allowed to be vulnerable, touching, being seen, sensual pleasure, confirmation of your attractiveness or soul presence. That which we yearn to experience in body, mind and soul can often carry an erotic charge.

Even when erotic love is fulfilled, its hot, saline pools never lie too far from the faultlines. The faultlines are the fine lines between pleasure and pain; the lines between pleasure and the fear pit of living ever unrequited.

The erotic world is a hot spring in the Lovelands where you must behave differently from other places; where you must let go of the other roles, other responsibilities and return to your essential self, cleansed of the world as you immerse yourself there. It's a wild place of freedom – it won't be constrained into someone else's plan, tidied into order, resolved for the sake of convenience or intellect. It bubbles deliciously, in view of Mount Danger, warmed by the same geothermal energy; but here that energy emerges from the ground as healing water instead of lava and fumes. Still, the waters are powerful: cover over the hot spring and it will find its way to the surface again through another hotspot, another opening in the ground of your being.

The tension of needing to bathe in the hot springs resets every time you leave, naked, wet and revitalised. Even as you dry yourself you can be planning when to immerse yourself again.

Returning again and again to the hot springs of your erotic imagination revitalises every part of your world. Perhaps you sometimes catch a glimpse of the faultlines as you bathe. The faultlines can become ancient monuments you rarely visit, whose wisdom you can honour, without having to descend into their shadows every day, forever.

Focus on the three great loves, let them be your compass. Base your decisions upon them, plan your days around them. Live for them. They will keep your course true. They will keep you whole.

21

WHOLE LOVE

The deepest possible presence is Love, and it begins with loving yourself, meeting yourself exactly where you are, kneeling to your own divinity and mothering your demons.

DANIELLE LAPORTE

Six months into our relationship, Andrew took me to Fiji and chartered a catamaran to a tiny, uninhabited island in the middle of the Pacific, as though we were the only two people on earth. He dropped to his knees on the beach, brought out a huge diamond ring that had been his mother's, pushed it onto my finger and asked me to marry him. It was that simple. My three great loves – relationships, self-acceptance and flow came together as we kissed, laughed and cried on the beach. My most longed-for desires became an unsurpassable reality and that tiny Fijian cove, bright with coral and teeming with life, became my Whole Love Harbour.

We married about a year after we'd met, amongst a group of friends, our kids beside us. I have three sons now and the most wonderful daughter. I call him the funniest man in the world. Life is more than beautiful.

~

On a rainy afternoon on the couch, Andrew and I talked about this book and I said that it was high time I completed it after a long process of pulling it together and making sense of the experiences and stories I wanted to share. We discussed how people's faultlines remain as underlying vulnerabilities, despite their healing, the distance of time and the wisdom of experience.

Andrew being a geologist, I'd assumed that the faultlines metaphor would really work to explain the psychology to him. It did, but not as I'd expected. He quietly chewed my ideas over for a while, then he said, 'But not all faults are weak. That's not *necessarily* the way faults work.'

'But the crack's always going to be there in the bedrock …'

'Yes, the fault is there, but it's not necessarily a vulnerability or a weakness.'

'What do you mean?'

'Well, there's this phenomenon called strain hardening,' he said, shifting into academic mode. 'It means the fault can actually become a zone of greater strength due to the changes in the rock. New minerals fill the fault and mend it with tougher material than the surrounding rock and bond it together at the same time. Sometimes the more strain there is, the harder the rock becomes, so these faults can form prominent ridges that are much harder than the surrounding rocks.'

I was dumbfounded with metaphoric possibility. 'Really?'

'Really. A fault can actually become a new outstanding landform after the rest of the landscape is well worn down because it's made of stuff that's much stronger than what was there before.'

I got it. Revelation.

'I love it!' I exclaimed, and happy tears inadvertently started to flow.

Andrew was a bit confused at my crying but I was jubilant and mid-epiphany. He hadn't quite finished the geology lecture.

'... and y' know what?'

'What?'

'The hardened fault often becomes a really striking and interesting feature of the landscape, almost to the point that sometimes the fault is the actual landmark you go to see, amongst all the surrounding stuff. The fault is the interesting, defining bit. I can show you one here, in the outback ...' He grabbed his iPad and started Googling images. 'Fountain Range. Here, here's a photo.'

Andrew had no idea of the gravity of what he had just given me. Here I was, suddenly wiser, with my psychological perspective and its metaphors massively improved by a bit of earth science from the big straight-up bloke.

'Why are you crying?' he asked. 'What have I done?'

'What you said was one of the most insightful, comforting things ever.' Tears rolled off my chin and plopped onto my chest. 'Where exactly is this range?' I asked. 'We should go there and have a look.'

'I'll show you on the map,' he said, pulling me and the iPad closer. 'It's not exciting country around there, just scrubby.' He showed me a picture of typical outback Australia – red dirt, grass, gum trees and rocks.

'I've been to worse places,' I said. 'It's no badlands.'

'Where's the badlands?' he asked.

'In the past,' I said.

～

Your faultlines don't leave you in one lifetime. They're part of your landscape. They're in your cells, so once you know them and get your head around their influence in your life, it's up to you how you regard them and how often you visit them. It's a choice to call them beautiful, benign ancient monuments in the valleys of your Lovelands – or to see them as dangerous, active and deadly. Life is less about what happens to you than it is about how you respond to what happens to you.

No one escapes suffering. You are not a victim of life and loss, unless you say you are. The faultlines hunger and gape – not to be filled by the love of another, but for you to bring peace to yourself, filling your insides with soul acceptance, good relationships and flow.

You are the ground of your being. The fact that you have faultlines means you are part of the very earth – ancient, strong, essential.

We fear falling into our faults' crevasses and suffocating in the darkness and dirt. However, when we sink into our faultlines' warm, thick scars and trust we will survive, there is relief in accepting who we are, faults and all, and how strong we can be under pressure. What we actually find ourselves in is not a crevasse but the depth of our being – everything built stronger around our scars. The deeper the hole, the deeper we can go, the closer to bone, the closer to home.

I wish you emotional freedom. I wish you self-love, a passionate life, and I send you my love.

Acknowledgements

Thank you to all at Hardie Grant – Fran Berry, Pam Brewster, Meelee Soorkia and Roxy Ryan, just to name a few. I'm so grateful for all your wonderful help. Fran, it was so easy to entrust the book to you wholeheartedly.

Nadine Davidoff – my editor from the start, you gave me the encouragement I needed as well as brilliant guidance all the way – unending gratitude to you.

Thank you to Mum for all you've done over the years to support my journeys near and far.

Thank you to my children and my husband, Andrew. You are my world.

Psychologist, couple therapist and former university lecturer in marriage and relationships, Debra Campbell has worked in private practice, consulting on everything from panic to depression and parenting problems. For a number of years she was a couple therapist at Relationships Australia.

Prior to psychology Debra taught yoga and meditation, so mindfulness remains a cornerstone of her work in mental health and couple relationships. She was the director of Hobsons Bay Yoga and Natural Health and Newport Yoga Centre. Her research has been published in psychological journals in Australia and the USA.

Debra lives in Melbourne, Australia, with her husband, kids and a dog. She can be found online at drdebracampbell.com.

The River
of Life

The Resilience
Retreat

The Plains
of Uncertainty

Hot
Springs

Broken Heart Beach

Mt Danger

The Mirages

Projection Pass

The Bay of
Bliss Dreams

LOVELANDS

Ground Zero